Psychic Voyages

Psychic Voyages
by Stuart Holroyd

⚂ Aldus Books London

Series Coordinator: John Mason
Design Director: Günter Radtke
Picture Editor: Peter Cook
Editor: Sally Burningham
Copy Editor: Mitzi Bales
Research: Marian Pullen
General Consultant: Beppie Harrison

EDITORIAL CONSULTANTS:

COLIN WILSON
DR. CHRISTOPHER EVANS

SBN 490 00347 8

© 1976 Aldus Books Limited London

First published in the United Kingdom
in 1976 by Aldus Books Limited
17 Conway Street, London W1P 6BS

D. L.: S.S.: 316/76

Printed and bound in Spain
by TONSA San Sebastián
and RONER Madrid

**Frontispiece: artist's impression of the astral body.
Above: the birdlike soul of ancient Egyptian belief.**

Psychic Voyages

Is our physical form merely a temporary casing for our true self? Many believe that it is, and that they have experienced different levels of reality by means of out-of-the-body projections. This book traces the history of astral projection and examines the evidence for it in the present scientific investigations.

Contents

1

Other Places, Other Times, Other Lives

One day in 1828 Robert Bruce, the first mate on a ship trading between Liverpool, England and Canada, saw a complete stranger seated in the captain's cabin, writing on a slate. The man turned and gazed at him with such a fixed grave expression that Bruce took alarm and rushed up on deck to report what he had seen to the captain.

"You must be going crazy, Mr. Bruce," said the captain. "A stranger and we are nearly six weeks out! Go down and see who it is."

"I never was a believer in ghosts," said Bruce, "but, if the truth must be told, sir, I'd rather not face it alone." So the captain and

This vision of one universe suspended inside another, entitled *Universes No.* 2, was painted by the psychic Ingo Swann, who claims to have explored space in the astral body. Many of his paintings portray the dazzling wonders of the universe as he has experienced them. In this painting, the clouds and hills represent the physical universe, and the stars the psychic universes. His goal in painting, he said in an interview for *Psychic*, is "to recreate in the minds of others certain conditions of existence or awareness that I have experienced."

"He had dreamed he was on a ship that was coming to their rescue"

mate went down together to the cabin, only to find it empty. When they examined the slate, however, they found written on it the words, "Steer to the Nor'west."

"Have you been trifling with me, sir?" said the captain sternly. Bruce swore that he had told the exact truth. The captain sat at his desk and pondered deeply for some minutes. Then he turned the slate over and asked Bruce to write "Steer to the Nor'west" on it. Satisfied that the writing on the two sides of the slate was completely different, he sent for the second mate and the steward in turn, and had them write the words. In this way he tested the entire crew. Not one of them had handwriting remotely resembling that on the slate. The ship was thoroughly searched from stem to stern, but no sign of a stowaway was found. "Mr. Bruce, what the devil do you make of all this?" the captain finally asked.

"Can't tell, sir," said Bruce. "*I* saw the man write; *you* see the writing. There must be something in it."

Because the wind was favorable and a detour would only lose them a few hours, the captain gave orders to change course to the northwest. After some three hours of sailing, the lookout reported an iceberg ahead with a ship close to it. When they drew closer, the captain saw through his glass that the ship, with many people aboard, was virtually a wreck and frozen fast in the ice. He sent out boats to rescue the survivors. When the third rescue boat returned and its occupants were ascending the ship's side, the mate was astonished to see among them the man he had seen in the captain's cabin some hours before.

"Upon my word, Mr. Bruce, this gets more and more singular," said the captain when the mate identified their new passenger. "Let us go and see this man."

At the captain's request, the man wrote the words, "Steer to the Nor'west," on the blank side of the slate, and he was as astonished as anyone when the slate was turned over and the same words in the same handwriting were found on the other side.

"I only wrote one of these. Who wrote the other?" he said, turning the slate over and over. He had no recollection of the event that had so alarmed Bruce, but he remembered an incident that could have been connected. That day at about noon he had fallen into a deep sleep of exhaustion, and when he awakened he had announced that he was sure they would all be saved that day, because he had dreamed he was aboard a ship that was coming to their rescue. The captain of the wrecked ship confirmed this story. "He described her appearance and rig," the captain said, "and, to our utter astonishment, when your vessel hove in sight she corresponded exactly to his description of her."

This story, published in Robert Dale Owen's *Footfalls on the Boundary of Another World* in 1860, was related to that author by Captain Clarke, a close friend of Robert Bruce's. He described Bruce as "as truthful and straightforward a man as ever I met in all my life," and told Owen, "I'd stake my life upon it that he told me no lie." It is certainly an extraordinary story, but it is typical of thousands that collectively add up to substantial evidence for one of the strangest and most incomprehensible of human abilities: the ability to travel out of the body to distant locations. The evidence comes from all over the world and from all periods of human history. Some cultures have accepted out-of-the-body, or astral, projection and have found explanations for its occurrence, but until recently the West had generally dismissed the phenomenon as hallucination, or shrugged it off as fantasy or superstition.

It seems that people of all ages and from all walks of life have had out-of-the-body experiences. In fact, statistical surveys suggest that out-of-the-body experiences, or OOBEs as they are generally referred to in writings about them, occur to as many as one person in five. Usually the phenomenon comes at a time of crisis, but sometimes it happens spontaneously and for no apparent reason. Such experiences cannot be dismissed as mere hallucination or fantasy because in some cases the person is seen by others while he or she is out of the body, or is able to offer some verifiable evidence of the astral journey.

A woman who lived in Ireland, for example, and was in the habit of projecting out of her body, located the house of her dreams on one of her trips. Over a period of a year she returned to it many times, and each time it pleased her more. She and her husband were planning to move, and she thought the house would suit them ideally if only she knew where it was. They went house-hunting in London—on the ordinary physical plane—and to her delight one advertisement they answered took them to the house she knew so well. Everything down to the furniture and the decorations was as she had seen it on her out-of-the-body trips. Furthermore, the place was remarkably cheap because it was said to be haunted. When the prospective buyer met the owner, the latter stared at her and screamed, "You're the ghost!"

Most OOBEs are simple experiences of what is known as *autoscopy*—that is, seeing oneself from a distance. The view is normally from above and usually occurs during sleep, frequently after childbirth or an operation. Those who experience it are always firmly convinced that they have seen themselves as never before, clearly, distinctly, vividly, and in detail from outside. Traveling OOBEs are rarer, but a considerable number of psychically gifted people have developed in themselves the facility to practice astral projection. The OOBE, whether it occurs only once and spontaneously or frequently and deliberately, always leaves those who have it with the conviction that they possess a second body or double that is not subject to the limitations of the physical body. Most become convinced that some kind of personal identity or consciousness survives death.

Space, time, and mortality are the fundamental limiting principles of physical existence. Basing our idea of reality on the testimony of our senses, we have come to believe that we can only be in one place at a time and can obtain first-hand information only about the present moment. We also think that the physical body is like a machine that gradually runs down and finally stops functioning altogether. Religions and esoteric philosophies of mankind have always held that there are planes of reality beyond the physical where the limiting principles of space, time, and mortality do not apply. But common sense has generally scoffed at this view as wishful thinking. Strangely enough, modern developments in physics, psychology, and philosophy have tended to lend support to the religious and esoteric view, and to oust common sense from its position as

Paul Twitchell is one of the many people who have claimed the ability to project the astral body, which he calls "Eckankar" or "soul travel." His writings have won him a large following in Europe and America, and many of his adherents claim that he has visited them astrally and cured them of illness or saved them from danger. Twitchell sees himself as standing at the hub of a spiritual wheel, sending cosmic power to his pupils at the rim of the wheel via "spiritual lines" represented by spokes.

9

supreme arbiter of what is real. Some experts say today that our senses were not evolved to give us knowledge of the Universe, but to enable us to exist within our environment. Their main function is to reduce the amount of confusing miscellaneous information that surrounds us, and to enable us to select what we need for practical survival.

If we accept the possibility of nonphysical planes of existence, the question then arises as to how we can gain information that would provide the proof about it. There have always been people claiming that they have special access to these nonphysical planes: shamans, witch doctors, mediums, mystics, psychics, and sensitives, for example. They have been regarded at different times and by different cultures either as demigods or frauds. Western scientists have recently begun to investigate their claims more seriously, and one of the areas of systematic and intensive scrutiny has been out-of-the-body experience. If people can really transcend the limitations of space, time, and mortality the implications for science, for philosophy, and for life are immense.

The flyer.

Left: an American Indian shaman or magician-priest-doctor, in a 16th-century view. Humans longing to escape the confines of the earthbound physical body is often expressed subconsciously in dreams of flying. The shaman deliberately induces a trancelike state in which he seems to leave his body. He dons a feathered costume and imitates the movements of birds in an attempt to become, in spirit, like a bird and to free his soul from physical limitations.

Above: in this painting a Tartar shaman dances around a fire to induce ecstasy. Among the peoples of central Asia shamanism is widespread. The shaman is believed to be capable of leaving his body at will. He does this for one or more of these purposes: to meet God face to face and bring Him an offering from the people; to increase his knowledge through contact with higher beings; to seek the soul of a sick person—it being believed that illness is caused by the "rape of the soul"; and to guide the soul of a dead person to its new abode. Shamans are also credited with other powers, such as turning themselves into animals and foretelling the future.

Left: the late Eileen Garrett, one of the foremost mediums of this century, who experienced astral projection on several occasions.

Right to far right: target drawings and response drawings by Ingo Swann from the ASPR experiment shown above. Target drawings are marked N (north) and S (south) to indicate their placement on the platform and so suggest the point of view from which Swann saw them. This was one of a series of such experiments which indicated that Swann could see, psychically, the target drawings—by either clairvoyance, telepathy, or out-of-the-body vision. By signaling when he had returned to the body, Swann helped experimenters detect changes in brain activity during the event.

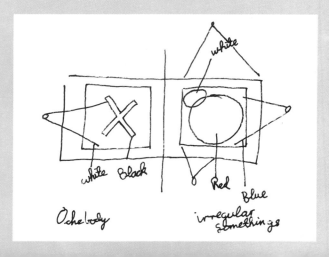

Left: during an experiment for the American Society for Psychical Research, Ingo Swann sits beneath a suspended platform on which two target pictures have been placed. He is attempting to project his consciousness up to the ceiling and so view the pictures lying on the platform. Electrodes stuck to his head measure Swann's brain activity.

Below: psychical researcher Janet Mitchell, one of the scientists who tested Swann at the ASPR. She stands beside a polygraph machine, which records subtle physical changes in the subject.

Some years ago a famous experiment was conducted with Mrs. Eileen Garrett, a medium who was highly respected by scientists because she took a serious approach to the study of her paranormal abilities. Eileen Garrett was able to project out of her body at will in a trance state, and to report on what she saw. In this particular experiment she was in an apartment in New York with a secretary and a psychiatrist. The target point for her projection was the office of a doctor in Reykjavik, Iceland. The doctor had assembled a number of objects on a table in his office, which the medium was to attempt to describe. She not only described the objects correctly, but also repeated word for word a passage from a book that he was reading at the moment, and reported that the doctor's head was bandaged. Both the passage from the book and the fact that he had a head injury just before the experiment took place were later confirmed by the doctor, who also said that he had sensed the presence of Mrs. Garrett in his office during the experiment.

A present-day psychic who both projects out of his body at will and at the same time reports on his experience is the New York artist Ingo Swann. Swann has demonstrated OOB perception over both long and short distances. Under controlled laboratory conditions he has projected out of the body to the ceiling and correctly identified objects and geometrical shapes placed on a platform well above his head. In his autobiography *To Kiss Earth Good-Bye*, he gives some examples of a type of astral projection experiment he devised himself. The target was not a physical object but a location on the earth's surface identified by its latitudinal and longitudinal coordinates. Swann would sit in a chair smoking a cigar, and an experimenter would give him a randomly chosen coordinate that he would attempt to probe psychically. For instance, given the coordinate 32°E and 30°N, he responded: "Ah, looks dry, like Italy, no, not Italy, what are those things in the far distance, ah, they look like Pyramids, is that Cairo?" The coordinate was, in fact, of a situation near Cairo.

In another experiment Swann was given the coordinate 49°20'S and 70°14'E, and he responded: "I see what seems to be a mountain sticking up through some clouds, no, not just a mountain, it must be an island." The experimenter said he was wrong and that the location was right in the middle of the southern Indian Ocean. Further checking revealed, however, that there was an island at the indicated location, with moun-

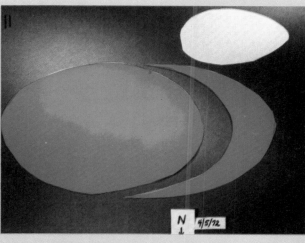

tains rising at its Eastern end. Swann continued his psychic probe, and drew a sketch of a part of the island showing a small landing field, some buildings, and some boats docked at a single jetty that had a lighthouse at its farther end. His sketch was later found to correspond with the features of the part of the island indicated by the coordinate, where a meteorological station was situated. This type of OOBE is called "remote viewing."

In 100 such experiments Swann gave 43 exactly correct descriptions of the location, and 32 descriptions that were nearly correct. He had 19 failures, and the remaining 6 were unverifiable. The tests were conducted under the supervision of Dr. H. Puthoff, a physicist of the Stanford Research Institute in California. He is typical of the new generation of scientists who are studying paranormal phenomena seriously, and believe they may provide the key for a future scientific revolution as radical as the revolutions that stemmed from the discoveries and theories of Copernicus, Newton, and Einstein. Puthoff has carried out a number of OOB tests with several psychically gifted subjects, among them a former police commissioner, Pat Price. In one series of tests with Price as the subject, a group of experimenters drove to a randomly selected location in the San Francisco area and remained there for half an hour. Price attempted to project himself to the place they had gone, and to describe the location. When independent judges were given his and the experimenters' separate descriptions, they were able to match six out of nine of them correctly. Price was also successful in projecting to an island in the Indian Ocean, reporting that while there in his second body he had heard people speaking French.

Thousands of accounts of OOBEs have been collected and analyzed by the English researcher Dr. Robert Crookall. Over several decades he has carefully investigated, checked, and collated accounts from correspondents from all over the world. Here is a typical case from his records.

A young Englishwoman had just gotten married and was traveling with her husband on a transatlantic liner to the United

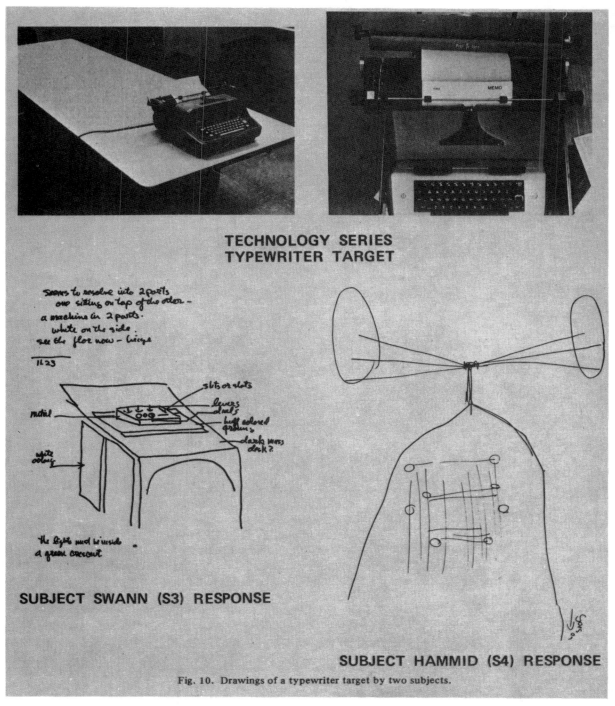

TECHNOLOGY SERIES
TYPEWRITER TARGET

Seems to resolve into 2 parts
one sitting on top of the other —
a machine in 2 parts.
white on the side.
see the floor now — beige

1123

slots or slots

levers
dials

buff colored
gadgets

dark mass
dark?

metal

white oblong

the light med to inside
a green crescent

SUBJECT SWANN (S3) RESPONSE

SUBJECT HAMMID (S4) RESPONSE

Fig. 10. Drawings of a typewriter target by two subjects.

Above: results from one series of remote viewing experiments conducted by Targ and Puthoff at SRI. The targets used were a group of machines located within the institute, and the one chosen for a given experiment was unknown to the experimenter sitting with the subject. The other experimenter would use the machine during a specified 15-minute interval while the subject attempted to reproduce it in a drawing and describe it on a tape recording. One of the psychically gifted subjects, Ingo Swann, achieved a close match. The other subject, Mrs. Hella Hammid, drew something that looked more like a uniform, but suggested the machine's keys and carriage.

Above: Alex Tanous, an American of Lebanese parentage, apparently possesses a great many psychic gifts, including the ability to leave the physical body and travel not only in space but also in time. Occasionally people have claimed to have seen him and even talked with him while he was physically in another place. While under observation in a laboratory he has projected himself into another room and moved an object inside that room.

States, where they were going to live. She was terribly seasick during the first day of the voyage. Her mother, sitting in her kitchen in England, was thinking about her daughter at the time. Suddenly she felt that she was out of her body and flying over the ocean. Finding the ship and the right cabin, she went in, took her daughter's hand, and told her that she would feel better if she washed, dressed, and went on deck. Then she flew back home. She noticed that only five minutes had elapsed since she had had the sensation of leaving her body. A few days later she received a letter from her daughter that confirmed every detail of the strange meeting: the time it had occurred, the condition the daughter had been in, and the exact words the mother had spoken to her.

Tales like this generally bring forth a polite smile, an unbelieving shrug, or an exclamation of "Incredible!" But the systematic and controlled research that parapsychologists and physicists are devoting to OOBEs today is steadily reducing their improbability. If just for the sake of an experiment a man can leave his physical body, project to a distant island he didn't know existed, and come back with an accurate description of it and its inhabitants, it is not at all improbable that a mother, strongly motivated by love and anxiety, might go out of the body to give comfort and help to her daughter at a time of distress.

Space is reportedly the limitation most easily and commonly transcended in OOBEs, and most accounts of such experiences record perception of events remote from where the physical body is situated. There is evidence, however, that the limitations of time can also be transcended in the OOBE. The following is an account of an experience by one of the best-known of all astral projectors, Sylvan Muldoon:

"In the spring of 1927, I awakened one night in the astral and found myself in a strange place—an unusually attractive park. I looked about me, observed its characteristics, and noted many special features, as well as its general aspect. I noted particularly a high rocky wall, and two small bridges crossing a stream. I had no memory of ever having visited this particular place, nor did I know where the place was. . . . It was two months later when, on a trip with a friend, I accidentally entered a park in a town about 50 miles from my home, and discovered it was the same place I had formerly visited in the astral!"

OOB time travel is a specialty of Alex Tanous, a present-day psychic who has on several occasions helped the police solve crimes and find missing persons, supposedly by projecting back in time and picking up a trail of events from the place where a person was last seen. At a meeting of psychologists, he once projected back to Russia at the time of the Revolution, and gave a vivid description of scenes and events details of which were later verified. On another occasion he told an anxious young woman whose mother was in the hospital for an operation exactly what was going to happen. By projecting into the future and observing events in the hospital, he told the woman that her mother's ailment would turn out not to be cancer, that a small section of the right lobe of her lung would be removed, that the operation would last one hour and 45 minutes, and that she would be out of the hospital within 10 days. These details later proved right.

So-called "false arrival cases" afford curious evidence that someone's double can be ahead of his or her physical body in time. The great novelist Leo Tolstoy vouched for the reality of this phenomenon. When the famous medium Daniel Dunglas Home was visiting Russia, Tolstoy and his wife went to meet him at Saint Petersburg railroad station. They saw Home get off the train and walk rapidly away, totally ignoring them. Tolstoy's wife sent a note to his hotel expressing their disappointment at his strange conduct. The note was awaiting Home when he arrived by a train that came in three hours later than the one his double had arrived on.

False arrival cases are said to be particularly common in Norway, where apparently the appearance of a double some time before the person shows up in the flesh is so normal that it is often taken as a signal to start making coffee. Whatever the reason for the prevalence of this phenomenon in Norway—Crookall has suggested that "the high altitude ... with diminished supply of oxygen favors the release of the double"—it is not confined to natives of that country. In 1955 an American businessman, Erkson Gorique, landed at Oslo airport and asked a taxi driver to take him to the best hotel. He had never been in Norway before and knew no one there. Imagine his surprise when the reception clerk at the hotel he was taken to said, "I'm glad to see you again, Mr. Gorique. It's so good to have you back." Wherever he went he was recognized and greeted, and everyone was under the impression that he had been there some months before. A wholesaler he visited on business welcomed him warmly by name and said, "You were in such a hurry the last time that we were not able to conclude the final details of our business." When Gorique protested that he had never been to the country before, the wholesaler told him about the common Norwegian experience of the "Vardøger," or forerunner. He assured Gorique that his experience wasn't such a rare thing, and he shouldn't let it disturb him unduly.

Gorique had been contemplating his journey some months before, and it seemed that in doing so he had unwittingly projected his double.

All the evidence for the reality of OOBEs points to the fact that the physical body is but a container, an "envelope" as some have called it, and that the essential self is not necessarily identified with it. There are many accounts by people who have been close to death of leaving the shell of the body and looking down on it with total indifference—even with a sense of relief at being finally freed of its limitations. If we make the assumption that human personality and the physical body do not constitute an integral unit, but are two separable entities, it is theoretically possible that there might be circumstances in which a body might be a host to more than one personality. Furthermore, if human personality survives death it is conceivable that it might return to inhabit another physical shell after one has served its temporary purpose.

Take the case of the Brazilian girl Silvia, born in São Paulo in March 1963. She began to introduce Italian words into her speech at an early age, but although she had Italian ancestry three generations back, nobody in her family or environment

The Sublime Vision of a Drowning Man

One gray windy day in 1929 a man named Robert went for a swim in the ocean with a friend named Mildred. He had an extraordinary experience, which he related some years later.

The sea was rough that day and the current extremely strong. He was about to head for shore when he heard a faint cry from a frightened youngster clinging desperately to a board. Robert managed to reach him and hoist him onto the board just before he himself was overcome by a mountainous wave. He felt himself sinking.

Suddenly, he found himself high above the water and looking down upon it. The sky, which had been gray and menacing, glowed with a glorious light. Waves of color and music vibrated around him, and he felt an indescribable peace.

Then below him he saw his friend Mildred in a rowboat with two men. Floating near them was a limp and ungainly object that he recognized as his own body. He felt a great sense of relief that he no longer needed it. The men pulled the body out of the water and lifted it into the boat.

The next thing he knew, he was lying on the beach, cold and aching. He later learned that it had taken two hours to revive him. His help had saved the boy from drowning.

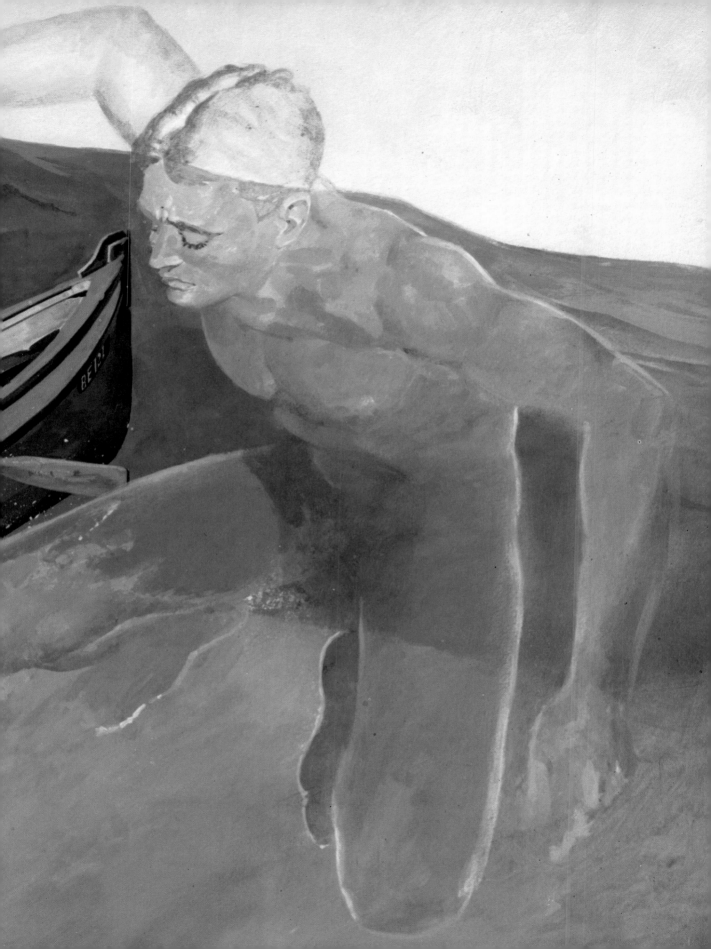

spoke Italian. It was her grandmother who first noticed Silvia's strange tendency, and from early in the child's life she kept a diary in which she noted the foreign words that Silvia came out with from time to time. She noted other things too. From the age of one month, Silvia manifested fear whenever an airplane flew overhead. Later when she was talking she referred to friends with Italian names, particularly one called Affonsa Dinari. One day when she was nearing her fourth birthday she happened to see a color photograph of Rome, and she said excitedly, "That's the Capitol. That's the house I used to live in, and that's the school, and those are the rocks I used to jump about on." The caption under the picture was simply "Rome, Italy," with no mention of the Capitol. When her family investigated further they found that what she had pointed out was indeed so named. On another occasion she told how she had died in her previous existence. A friend had run toward her carrying a bomb that looked like a fountain pen. The bomb had suddenly exploded. "My friend and me, we went up and up . . ." she said. When her grandmother asked her what had happened next, Silvia said, "Then I came here."

This is one of many cases that have been collected by the Brazilian Institute for Psycho-Biophysical Research, and seem to provide evidence for reincarnation. The staff of the Institute, headed by an electronics engineer, Hernani Andrade, have carefully checked out hundreds of cases of young children having knowledge that they could not have obtained by normal means. Investigating Silvia's story, for instance, they found that the Allies had in fact dropped bombs of a fountain pen type on Rome

Left: the Russian writer Leo Tolstoy who, along with his wife, saw the "false arrival" of D. D. Home at the St. Petersburg railroad station. Although born an aristocrat, with great wealth and property, Tolstoy turned in later years to a life of asceticism in keeping with his radical moral and religious thinking.

21

Left: in this Egyptian painting, the birdlike entity called the *ba* hovers over the mummified remains of the deceased. Ancient Egyptian concepts of the soul included other entities: one known as the *ka*, the person's double that lived on in the tomb and consumed the food left for it, and the *akh*, a spiritual power that came into existence at the point of death. Below: the Hindu god Vishnu is shown in this 18th-century painting, reincarnated as a white horse. This was supposedly his 19th reincarnation. Belief in reincarnation is fundamental to the Hindu religion, and many cases of people remembering previous lives have been reported and studied in India.

during World War II. A prominent member of the Institute writes: "Allowing for the creativity of childish imaginations, we consider that we have gathered good evidence showing that reincarnation is a probability worthy of very serious consideration."

The very idea of reincarnation may be distasteful to the modern rationalist view of reality, but it is a fundamental belief in most of the world's religions, and one that the great Western philosophers of the ancient world—Pythagoras, Socrates, and Plato—all believed in. The idea that humans have a second immortal body is also basic to the beliefs of Christianity. In rejecting the idea of reincarnation, rationalism is rejecting not only the beliefs of many of the great thinkers and leaders of mankind throughout history, but also those of a steadily increasing number of present-day scientists. When the great accumulation of evidence from a wide variety of sources is seriously investigated, a philosophy that holds space, time and mortality as absolute limiting principles begins to look questionable.

Above: Hernani G. Andrade, founder and president of the Brazilian Institute for Psycho-Biophysical Research. An engineer and former civil servant, Mr. Andrade has made an extensive study of psychic phenomena and investigated many cases of apparent reincarnation—a belief that is prevalent among the people of Brazil.

2

Theories From the Past

Reports suggest that United States and Soviet government agencies have been vying with each other for years to develop methods of psychic espionage. The idea of using astral projection to discover the enemy's closely guarded secrets may sound like something out of futuristic fiction but, according to some interpretations, it can actually be traced back to the Bible. The prophet Elisha in the *Second Book of Kings* is supposed to have used his psychic powers for just such a purpose.

Syria and Israel were at war. Time and again the Syrian king had selected a point to launch a surprise attack, only to find that the

Right: this early 19th-century miniature from the *Bhagavata Purana*, written around the 10th century, depicts a scene from the legend of Usha's dream flight. In the story the young woman has a spontaneous out-of-the-body experience, in which she visits a distant place and returns with information about it that can be objectively verified. A modern Indian religious teacher, Bhagwan Shree Rajneesh, believes that humans are composed of seven bodies, ranging from the physical body up to the Nirvanic, each capable of having its own dreams. Dreams of the more spiritual bodies are more likely to contain elements of reality, Rajneesh maintains, than are the familiar dreams of the physical body.

Israelites had moved their army to that very place and were well-prepared to defend it. The king's plans were made in the seclusion of his own bedchamber, so he began to suspect that one of his trusted advisers was passing secret information to the enemy. He called them together for questioning. One, bolder than the rest, stepped forward. He denied that any of them had been responsible for betraying the king, and he offered a new theory to account for the leakage of information. He told them of the strange psychic powers of the Israelite prophet Elisha. "Elisha the prophet that is in Israel telleth the king of Israel the words that thou speakest in thy bedchamber," he suggested.

The Syrian king seems to have accepted the idea that a man many miles away could, through some mysterious or magical power, discover the secret plans of his innermost council. He determined to capture the prophet, and sent a large expeditionary force to surround the town where he was living. However, once more he proved to be no match for Elisha. The prophet prayed to God, and the Syrian soldiers were struck blind. Elisha led them to the King of Israel, restored their sight, gave them food and drink, and sent them home. Not surprisingly, perhaps, they troubled Israel no more.

The story of Elisha suggests the interesting possibility that psychic powers had an early use in espionage. But not all such accounts that have come down to us from the Ancient World have had such a happy outcome. The story of Hermotimus of Clazomene, a Greek mystic of the 6th century B.C., is a cautionary tale. All psychic travelers in particular should bear it in mind.

Hermotimus was in the habit of spending days out of his body, roaming around the material and astral worlds. He would leave his physical body in the care of his wife, and when he returned to it he would tell her all about his adventures. His wife became rather bored with his tales and resentful of his long absences, and she decided to give him a shock. He had always stressed before his departures that if his physical body were moved at all he might have difficulty getting back into it. So she recruited two helpers, supposed friends of her husband's, to move his body to another room. Hermotimus' wife didn't doubt that he would be able to reenter his body, but she thought that if it were difficult this time, he might think twice before embarking on another excursion. What she didn't know was that the two supposed friends were in fact her husband's rivals in sorcery. They simply cremated his body. Hermotimus' ghost, it was said, hung about his home for years afterwards, wailing for restoration of the physical body he had been cheated of.

There is a belief found in many different parts of the world that in sleep a person travels out of his body. It is therefore thought to be dangerous to awaken a person too abruptly, because his traveling body may not have had time to get back into the physical one, and the two may be permanently separated.

The notion that man has more than one body, and that the physical is only one of several forms of existence, can be found in ancient cultures and religions all over the world. Long before Christianity people believed in the resurrection of the body after death, and in mystic journeys of the spirit during life. The Church Fathers waged a campaign against all forms of pagan super-

Left: a painting of the prophet Elisha raising the son of the Shunammite woman from the dead. Elisha was credited with the ability to travel astrally.
Below: a painting by Botticelli of St. Augustine (AD 354–430). A profound thinker and author of many books, including the *Confessions* and *The City of God*, Augustine believed in the possibility of out-of-the-body experiences and told a story of an OOBE yielding verifiable information.

Above: an 18th-century Jain icon in brass representing the spirit liberated from matter. Like Hinduism, the Jain religion teaches the transmigration of souls and the belief that eventually the soul can be freed from the cycle of rebirths. Appropriately, the liberated spirit—called the Jina or Victor in Jainism—is suggested in this icon by empty space.

Right: a representation of a tree spirit carved on the branch of a sacred tree in India. Animism, the belief that everything in nature has a spirit, is believed to be the first form of religion that primitive people develop.

stition and magic, but the ancient belief in astral travel was not regarded as a superstition. Saint Augustine tells a story that involves the acquisition of verifiable information during an out-of-the-body experience.

A senator by the name of Curma was near death, and after several days in a coma, his spirit separated from his body. He heard his name being called, and thought that he was being summoned for posthumous judgment. But he learned from other spirits that he was still alive and that it was another Curma, a goldsmith who had just died, who was being called. He noticed that not all the beings around him were spirits of the dead, because some were of people he knew to be still alive. If he himself were not dead, then, he and they must be on a visit to some limbo region. Finally he returned to his physical body, came out of his coma, and immediately sent someone to the house of Curma the goldsmith. The messenger returned with the news that the artisan had recently died.

The idea that humans have a second body that coexists with the physical one but can separate from it during life, particularly in conditions of trance or sleep, and survives it after death, arose very early and is widespread. It rests on the belief that everything has another reality apart from the reality it presents to our senses. According to this belief, there is another world, invisible and intangible but no less real, lying beyond the world we can see and touch. Nothing is what it seems. Trees, mountains, stones, plants, rivers, lakes—all have spirits. The stars and planets are living entities that influence life on earth, and the world is full of hidden mysterious forces and interactions. The essence of this belief, which we now call *animism*, was expressed as far back as the 6th century B.C. by one of the earliest Greek philosophers, Thales of Miletus. In his words, "All things are full of gods."

To the Western scientific mind of the 19th century, such a

Left: this wooden Eskimo salmon mask, worn at a spring festival, depicts not only the physical form of the fish but also the frightening spirit that lurks within it. The Eskimo religion is animistic, and contains many elements of fear. The spirits that inhabit all creatures are potentially menacing, and the spirits of humans that have died must be placated and guarded against by a host of taboos and special precautions.

statement seemed to be pure nonsense. Modern science was founded on the idea of the existence of an objective physical world that would yield its secrets to investigation by analysis and dissection, and on the belief that man, with his trained intellect and sophisticated tools, was equipped to discover ultimate truths. Its criteria of reality were clear. Everything existed in three-dimensional space; all matter was an aggregate of invisible atomic particles possessing mass and controlled by mechanical forces that obeyed fixed laws; every event must be causally linked with a prior one. Anything that failed to meet these criteria could not possibly be real. The ancient animist view of the world was rejected by 19th-century science as childish and ignorant.

In the present century, however, new scientific discoveries have reversed many of the notions of the 19th century, and the early animist ideas no longer appear entirely ridiculous. To the three dimensions of space Einstein has added time as a fourth dimension, and modern quantum theory postulates a multi-dimensional Universe. Mass has been shown to be a property of matter only at the macroscopic level, and even then to be convertible to energy. At the microscopic level mass disappears completely, and particles become waves. Other particles appear

Below: the ancient and widespread belief that all living things have a nonmaterial essence has received some scientific backing in recent years with the development of Kirlian photography. This process, the work of a Soviet scientist, reveals a glowing aura given off by animals and even plants, such as this daisy. Even when part of a leaf is cut away, the aura of the removed section will remain visible in the photograph.

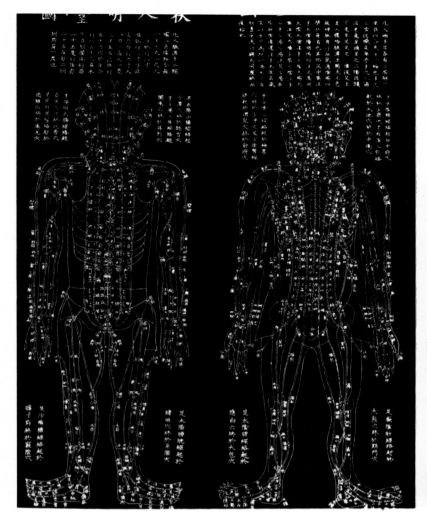

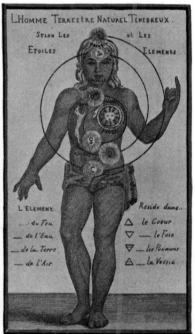

Left: an ancient Chinese chart showing the points for acupuncture, each associated with an organ of the body. The points are located along 12 lines, or meridians, through which the life force is believed to flow. Research into the aura shows that shafts of light are emitted from points corresponding to acupuncture points.

possessing illogical properties like negative mass or the ability to move backward in time. At this microscopic level, uncaused events constantly occur, effects sometimes precede causes, and mechanical laws break down and have to be replaced by mathematical laws of probability. Strange as it may seem, 20th-century physics has moved away from the scientific philosophy of the 19th century, and in many ways appears closer to the old animist view. Scientists examining the hierarchy of living organisms find it increasingly difficult to draw a line below which they can confidently assert that consciousness does not exist. Nothing is just what it seems. There appear to be other dimensions of reality not accessible to human senses.

Soviet scientists have in recent years been investigating the energy fields, or auras, that surround and emanate from living organisms. Mystics and sensitives throughout the ages have claimed to be able to distinguish an aura surrounding the physical body. Modern techniques of electrophotography have confirmed these claims. Photographs have established that a second body, often called a bioplasmic or energy body by scientists, does in fact surround the physical one. Even more, they confirm ancient theories about this aura. In the 2nd century A.D. the Greek writer Plutarch described how different kinds of

Above: this illustration from *Theosophica Practica*, a book by the 17th-century German mystic Johann Georg Gichtel, shows the seven chakras, which—according to Hindu belief—are located at points where the subtle body and the physical body are connected. The chakras are thought to be centers of psychic energy. Like the acupuncture points, they seem to correspond to the points where light is released in the aura.

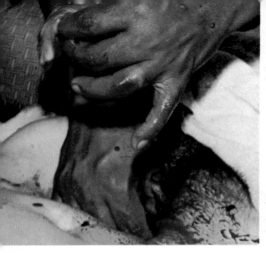

Left: Filipino "psychic surgeon" Tony Agpaoa, who performs what appear to be operations using only his bare hands to open the body. His 40-bed clinic receives patients from many countries.
Far left: an abdominal "operation" being performed by Agpaoa. Some observers have suggested that the blood and diseased tissue are produced by sleight of hand and that perhaps the healing reported by patients results from his having really operated on the subtle body.

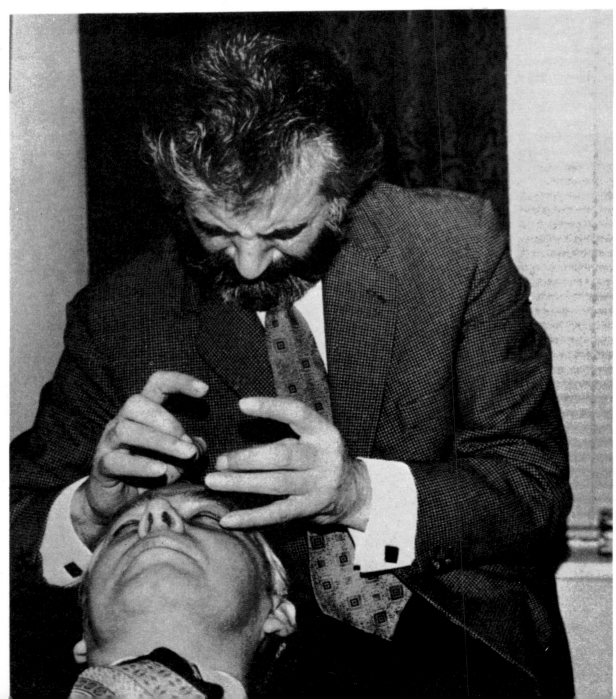

Above: William Lang, a British ophthalmologist and Fellow of the Royal College of Surgeons who died in 1937 but who—according to many people—is still operating on patients today, via the medium George Chapman. The spirit of Dr. Lang is reported to have successfully treated a great variety of ailments by operating on the patient's spiritual body.

Left: medium George Chapman doing a psychic eye operation while "controlled" by Dr. Lang. Chapman remains in a trance during the treatment and does not touch the patient. He maintains that illness results from the spirit self not being in harmony with the physical self. The spirit body, he says, supplies energy to the physical body. He admits that not all of the operations have been successful, but startling and apparently spontaneous cures are reported by many of the people who visit his clinic in Aylesbury.

human auras corresponded with different physical and psychological states. The Soviets have found that the light emitted by a living body is bright, dull, colorful, or colorless depending on the state of the person.

Another unexpected result of recent research into the aura is that the human body emits strange shafts of light from certain points, and these points seem to correspond exactly with the points used in the ancient Chinese technique of acupuncture. Acupuncturists believe that the body is traversed by a system of invisible meridian lines which carry the life force essential to the body's health. The insertion of needles at certain points along a meridian line will help cure discomfort or pain at other points along the line. Great skill is needed in order to select these points. Acupuncture is puzzling to those trained in Western medicine because the meridian lines and points do not correspond to any physical system in the body. They cannot be located by eye. The discovery that the points correspond to shafts of light in the human aura does, however, lend more credence to the suggestion that the acupuncturist may be operating on the subtle, or astral, body to cure the physical body.

The idea of the subtle body is widespread, but it is found especially in Eastern religions and occult beliefs. It is thought to be the ethereal and invisible counterpart, or double, of the physical body. It is said to be composed of semifluid matter and a network of ganglia, and is supposed to be separate from the physical body but meeting it at certain points. In yoga, the points at which the physical and subtle bodies meet are known as the chakras or wheels. They are thought to be psychic centers of superhuman energy. It has been found that the points at which the chakras are said to be located also correspond with shafts of light in the human aura.

In Brazilian Spiritist healing, operations are sometimes performed on the physical body and sometimes on the subtle body, also known as the perispirit. In the operations on the perispirit, the physical body is not touched. Guy Playfair, a present-day English psychic researcher who has lived in Brazil for many years, has witnessed operations of both kinds. In his recent book *The Flying Cow*, he describes the work of Edivaldo Silva, a schoolteacher who in his spare time as a spirit healer has treated about 65,000 patients in 10 years. Edivaldo told Playfair that when he operated he was in a trance state, and never remembered any of his patients later. He was controlled by a number of spirit doctors, but mainly by a Spanish-speaking one called Dr. Calazans.

When Playfair watched Edivaldo, controlled by Calazans, in action, he noticed that his voice and manner was different from when he was out of trance. Edivaldo was usually gentle and soft-spoken, but under Calazans' control was authoritative and brusque. In one operation witnessed by Playfair, the patient was a man aged about 30. He lay on a table with his shirt unbuttoned to expose his chest and stomach. Edivaldo-Calazans moved his hands about in the air above the man's stomach, keeping up a commentary as if for a class of medical students while he worked. At first Playfair caught only odd phrases such as ". . . separate the etheric double . . . fourth dimension . . . remove the plasma from the red corpuscles." Edivaldo-Calazans kept waving his

Above: an Eskimo shaman beats his drum during a Christmas celebration that still retains elements of the pagan festival it supplanted. The drum is one of the aids used by a shaman in his process of inducing a state of ecstasy so as to leave his physical body. In Eskimo belief, the shaman plays a vital role in placating the important spirits that control the natural world, for he can fly to their dwelling places and there perform the required rituals.

hands about. "Now he's feeling it open," he said. "Not in the mind, but in the body itself, above the stomach. . . . Now we are putting in a drain, to serve as tubing."

When the operation was over Edivaldo gave instructions that the patient rest completely for 48 hours; but it turned out that the man had brought nobody with him and had intended to drive himself home. Edivaldo was immensely amused at this and sent him to lie on another bed while he attended to the next patient. Playfair reports: "The man climbed stiffly off the bed and slumped onto the other bed. He looked dazed and weak. The whole operation had been entirely invisible to my eyes, but he had certainly felt something. He began to moan. . . ." He continued moaning and muttering incoherently to himself for a long time, and in an

interval between operations Edivaldo drew the onlookers' attention to him. "See the effect of the anesthetic?" he said. "Know what that is called? No? Shock, that's what. Anaphylactic, or postoperative shock." He ordered the man to sit up and drink some coffee, and told him he would shortly be well enough to go home by taxi.

Operations on the second body that cure the physical body are also regularly performed today by the English healer George Chapman. His control is Dr. William Lang, an eminent eye specialist who died in 1937. Bernard Hutton, a journalist who was cured of polio and incipient blindness by Chapman, has written a remarkable book, *Healing Hands*. He tells of numerous healings allegedly performed by Lang through Chapman, which have involved no contact between the healer and the patient's physical body. Evidence for the reality of second-body healing may not be conclusive, but it is certainly abundant.

Healing is also one of the chief functions of shamans, the magician-priests who still survive today in tribal communities from Australia to the Arctic. Shamans are believed to be able to leave their body at will, and to travel throughout the material world or the regions of the dead. They claim that there are spirits, gods, and demons that are responsive only to their powers. Besides curing sickness, the shaman directs communal sacrifices and escorts the souls of the dead to the other world. According to Professor Mircea Eliade, who has written a scholarly book entitled *Shamanism*, the shaman is able to do these things because he has mastered the techniques of ecstasy: "that is, because his soul can safely abandon his body and roam at vast distances, can penetrate the underworld and rise to the sky. Through his own ecstatic experience he knows the roads of the extraterrestrial regions. He can go below and above because he has already been there. The danger of losing the way in these forbidden regions is still great; but sanctified by his initiation and furnished with his guardian spirits, the shaman is the only human being able to challenge the danger and venture into a mystical geography."

The "techniques of ecstasy" are in fact the techniques of out-of-the-body projection. The word "ecstasy" means literally "standing outside," and the shaman achieves this trancelike state through dance, music, fasting, meditation, drug-taking, or self-hypnosis. In some tribal societies the shaman not only accomplishes the healing of ailments believed to be caused by "loss of

Above: spirits of an Eskimo shaman, drawn by the shaman himself. Some Eskimos believe that a person's soul is a kind of miniature of him that lives somewhere in his body. Others think that many of these souls are scattered around the body—particularly at the joints. Below: this 17th-century engraving shows a shaman of central Asia wearing a coat decorated with embroidery and a fringe of bones. In the young shaman's initiatory dream, he is dismembered by demonic beings, who scrape the flesh from his bones. The bones are then put back together and covered with new flesh. In Siberia it is believed that he is given the same number of spirits as there are bones left over after he has been reconstituted.

Above: Pluto and Persephone
pictured on a Greek amphora. According to mythology, Pluto—
also known as Hades—abducted
his niece Persephone and carried
her down to the shadowy underworld
in which he lived. This underworld
was conceived of as a gloomy
and marshy place crossed by several rivers, to which the souls
of the deceased would travel.

soul," but also practices divination and clairvoyance, and can
travel out of his body to locate lost objects, people, or animals.
Shamans are reputed to be able to cover vast distances in an
instant, to be in two places at the same time, and to visit places
inaccessible to ordinary mortals. Buddhist legend tells of the
miraculous lake Anavatapa, and Hindu legend of the mysterious
northern land Svetadvipa. Both are places that can only be
reached by those capable of magical flight. Legends of visits to
the underworld, which are common in Nordic and Greek mytho-
logies, are expressions of the shamanic tradition. Eskimo shamans claim to undertake fantastic journeys, remain out of the
body for days, and return to tell of adventures in the depths of
the sea or among the stars. During their flight their physical
bodies remain in a state of suspended animation, motionless and
apparently lifeless. Eliade says, "they always take the precaution
of having themselves bound with ropes, so that they will journey
only 'in spirit;' otherwise they would be carried into the sky and
would vanish for good."

One of the chief functions of the shaman is the guidance of
the souls of the dead. This role is particularly emphasized in
Lamaism, the Tibetan form of Buddhism. The famous *Tibetan
Book of the Dead* is a kind of guidebook to the afterworld, direct-
ing the departed soul as to which routes to travel and which to
avoid. The "science of death" is a complex science in Tibetan
tradition, and a dying man needs the assistance of highly trained
priests in order to accomplish the right manner of separation of
the soul from the physical body. The priest supervises the retreat
of consciousness in the dying man, making him focus attention on
each of his bodily functions and senses in turn and deliberately
relinquish them. He guides the departing soul into the summit of
the skull, and at the moment of death shouts the magic syllable

"Hik!" in order to open a hole in the skull through which the soul can depart. When the separation has been properly accomplished, the priests chant ritual texts to guide the soul on its way.

Strangely enough, neuroscientists studying the process of dying have discovered that consciousness gradually deserts the physical body, finally retreating into the fourth ventricle of the brain. This ventricle forms part of a complex that is the first internal body structure to appear in an embryo. It is as if the soul retreats by the way it came. Moreover, at the moment that consciousness finally deserts the fourth ventricle, the body loses about one-half to three-quarters of an ounce of weight. This is a phenomenon that has been known for 60 years but has never been explained in terms of loss of physical matter. Perhaps the Tibetan shamans

Above: a photo taken in the 1920s showing two Tibetan lamas wearing aprons made of human bones. A Jesuit missionary to Tibet in the 18th century reported that the Tibetans did not bury their dead, but fed the bodies to birds and other animals. This was an expression of their belief in the passage of souls from one creature to another and an affirmation of man's oneness with all of nature.

Right: a scene from the Indian epic *Mahabharata*, which tells of a war between two related royal families. One of the combatants, Drona, lays aside his armor and regrets that he, a Brahmin, has taken up arms and shed blood. He sits yogi-fashion under a tree and begins to collect his soul together from his limbs. As his head is cut off by the brother of a man he has killed, his soul rises up like a red flame. The story recalls the symbolic assistance given to the dying by Tibetan priests, who shout the magic syllable "Hik!" at the point of death in order to open the skull and enable the soul to pass through it.

Above: the elusive anthropologist and best-selling author Carlos Castaneda photographed in the research room of the UCLA library. His books about a Mexican Indian sorcerer called Don Juan, who initiated him into the world of drugs and magic, has sold hundreds of thousands of copies.

know certain things about death that surpass the scientific knowledge of the West.

In four books published since 1968, Carlos Castaneda, an American anthropologist who became apprenticed to a Mexican Indian sorcerer, shows that the shamanic tradition is still very much alive today. Even if his books were fictitious, as some critics have suggested, they would still constitute a brilliantly imaginative evocation of shamanism, and it does not seem too highly improbable that in Don Juan and Don Genaro the young anthropologist had the good fortune to meet and be taken into the confidence of two genuine modern shamans.

Toward the end of his first book, *The Teachings of Don Juan*, Castaneda describes an OOBE, and a subsequent discussion of it that he had with Don Juan. Don Juan had told him that a sorcerer can soar through the air for hundreds of miles to see what is happening or to strike a fatal blow to an enemy. After drinking a potion concocted by Don Juan from the root of datura, or devil's weed, Castaneda took off. He pushed up with both feet, sprang backward, and glided on his back. "I saw the dark sky above me, and the clouds going by me. I jerked my body so I could look down. I saw the dark mass of the mountains. My speed was extraordinary. My arms were fixed folded against my sides. My head was the directional unit. If I kept it bent backward, I made vertical circles. I changed direction by turning my head to the side. I enjoyed such freedom and swiftness as I had never known before. . . ." He finally descended and landed amid landscape he recognized as being about half a mile from Don Juan's house. He was completely naked and it was nearly dawn. He tried to run but hurt his feet on the stones of the road. He hid behind bushes when he saw someone approaching along the road, but when the figure drew closer he saw that it was Don Juan and that he was bringing his clothes.

The experience was unusually real and vivid, but was it an hallucination? "Did I really fly, Don Juan? . . . I mean, did my body fly? Did I take off like a bird?" Castaneda asked. Don Juan replied that the purpose of the devil's weed was for flying, so of course he had flown, and as he took more of it he would learn to fly perfectly. Castaneda wasn't satisfied. He asked if a friend would have been able to see him fly. That depended on the friend, Don Juan said. Exasperated, Castaneda asked what would have happened if he had been tied to a rock with a heavy chain. Don Juan was puzzled by his insistent questions, and answered that he would have to fly holding the rock with the heavy chain. He didn't understand Castaneda's problem, and his insistence on the word "really." The sorcerer's world was one of multileveled reality. "The trouble with you," he told his apprentice, "is that you understand things in only one way."

Castaneda gave up his apprenticeship after some frightening experiences that made him fear for his sanity and his life, but he couldn't stay away for long from the strange world of adventure and knowledge that Don Juan had introduced him to. He later met Don Juan's friend and fellow-sorcerer Don Genaro, an ebullient old man full of clownish humor in whose presence he always "experienced the most outlandish sensory distortions." At the beginning of his fourth book, *Tales of Power*, Castaneda relates one of his weirdest experiences. Don Juan was supervising him in some exercises in intense visualization. He called up before his mind's eye images of 32 persons in succession. Don Juan told him that to conclude he should try to call up Don Genaro. Castaneda went through the prescribed procedure, and suddenly Don Genaro was standing in front of him, large as life. "You called me, didn't you?" he said "Where were you?" Castaneda asked. He was sure that the two old men must have contrived an elaborate trick just to astonish him. But Don Genaro replied that he had been in his home in central Mexico several hundred miles away when Castaneda had called him. Don Juan explained in a matter-of-fact manner that, "Genaro is a man of knowledge. . . . And being a man of knowledge, he's perfectly capable of transporting himself over great distances." He went on to say that consummate sorcerers were capable of being in two places at once. "For a warrior like Genaro," he said, "to produce the other was not such a far-fetched enterprise."

The Devil's Weed

For more than two years, the young anthropology student had been apprenticed to the old Indian and had learned from him many strange secrets about the desert. Then one day the Indian, Don Juan, told him that it was time to test the Devil's weed. The student, Carlos, gathered the plants. Under the Indian's direction he laboriously concocted a paste from the roots of the plants, and finely ground seeds and insects. Don Juan then prepared a potion, which he told Carlos to drink. It made the young man's heart pound. Don Juan ordered him to smear the paste over his naked body.

The smell suffocated him, but he obeyed. When he tried to walk he discovered that his legs were "rubbery and . . . extremely long." He moved forward and then soared into the air. He glided effortlessly among the clouds. "The marvelous darkness gave me a feeling of sadness, of longing . . . as if I had found a place where I belonged. . . ."

Suddenly he knew that it was time to come down. He descended with slow, jerky motions that nauseated him, and he lost consciousness. When he came to, he was lying naked, about half a mile from Don Juan's house. He saw a man coming toward him, carrying clothes. It was Don Juan.

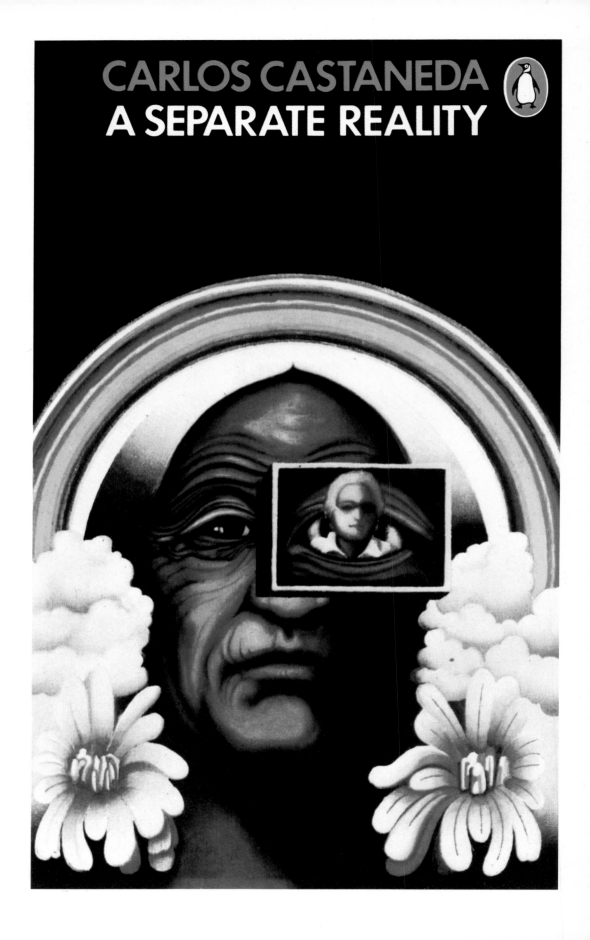

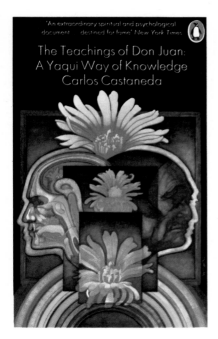

Above: the cover of Castaneda's first book, in which he describes meeting the Yaqui sorcerer and his own apprenticeship with him. Left: in this second book Castaneda describes how Don Juan taught him to "see" reality— that is, to experience the world directly, without interpreting it—through the aid of drugs. Below: his third book tells how Castaneda learned to "see" without drugs, through meditation and exercises in perception.

Castaneda was full of questions, which Don Juan answered patiently.

"Is the other like the self?"

"The other is the self."

"What's the other made of?"

"There's no way of knowing that."

"Is it real or just an illusion?"

"It's real of course."

"Would it be possible to say that it is made of flesh and blood?"

"No. It would not be possible."

"But you have to admit, Don Juan, that there must be a way to know."

"The double is the self; that explanation should suffice. If you would *see*, however, you'd know that there is a great difference between Genaro and his double. For a sorcerer who *sees*, the double is brighter."

Don Juan said that in all the years Castaneda had known Don Genaro, he had only been with the original Genaro twice, and every other time he had been with his double.

"But this is preposterous," Castaneda said.

Don Juan said, "I've told you time and time again that the world is unfathomable. And so are we, and so is every being that exists in this world. It is impossible, therefore, to reason out the double. You've been allowed to witness it, though, and that should be more than enough."

Castaneda was understandably astonished by his experience of calling up Don Genaro's palpable and physical double, and bewildered by Don Juan's explanation. His readers no doubt share his bewilderment and incredulity. But tales of the appearance of a person's double in solid corporeal form are so common the world over, and in many cases so well authenticated, that the phenomenon, inexplicable though it is, has to be taken seriously. Such tales are even found in the annals of governments. For example, a member of the British House of Commons, Dr. Mark Macdonell, appeared in the House in his double and cast a vote on an important measure when his other body was confined to his bed because of a serious illness. Another member of the august assembly, Sir Carne Rasch, was seen in the House by other members during an important discussion in 1908, although at the time he was laid up with influenza. A member of the Legislative Council of British Columbia, Charles Good, was not only seen by other members but also photographed with them in January 1865, though he was gravely ill at home and possibly in a coma. Politicians are not normally accomplished in the art of sorcery—at least in the strict meaning of the term—and one would not look among their number for adepts of second-body projection. Evidence for the reality of the human double among them, then, is most unexpected.

The Catholic Church has always accepted that bilocation, or being in two places at once, and astral travel are possible, though with the reservation that only individuals of great sanctity are capable of achieving these powers. Such a man was Saint Anthony of Padua. According to tradition, while he was preaching in a church in Limoges in 1226, he suddenly remembered that he was supposed to be present at that moment at a service in a

43

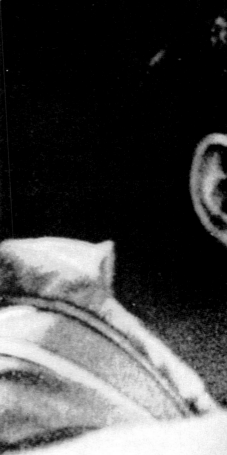

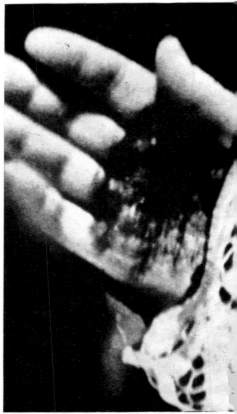

church on the other side of town. He interrupted his sermon, knelt down, and drew his hood over his head. For several minutes the congregation waited patiently for him to resume, assuming that he was praying. Meanwhile, in the other church, monks saw the saint appear among them, heard him read an appointed passage in the service, and then witnessed his sudden disappearance. His double returned to his original body, and the first sermon was resumed.

Saint Alphonsus Liguori came round from a five-day fast and trance one autumn day in 1774, and told the friars assembled around him that he had been out of his body and had attended at the deathbed of Pope Clement XIV. News of the Pope's death had not reached the monastery at the time, because Rome was four days' journey away. His statement was later confirmed by people who had been at the bedside of the dying pope. They said they had seen him there, kneeling in prayer.

The tales of Saints Anthony and Alphonsus may be no more than legends, but there are people living today who can testify to the ability of the Capuchin monk Padre Pio to materialize from nowhere, and help people in trouble. Padre Pio hardly ever left his monastery near Poggia, Italy, but his busy double was out healing and helping all over the place. During World War I an Italian general, after a series of defeats, was on the point of committing suicide when a monk entered his tent and said, "Such an action is foolish," and promptly left. The general didn't hear of the existence of Padre Pio until some time later, but when he visited the monastery near Poggia, he identified him as the monk

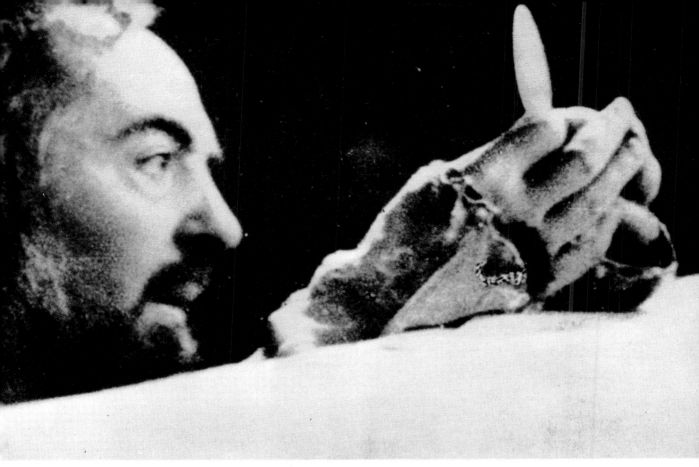

Above: the late Padre Pio celebrating Mass. The Italian priest was widely loved and venerated, and many people have told stories of his out-of-the-body visits to people who were suffering or in danger when he appeared to them.

Left: Padre Pio's hand, showing one of the stigmata that appeared when he was 31 years old. He was praying before the altar of his church when suddenly he cried out and collapsed, unconscious. His fellow friars ran to his aid and found him bleeding from his hands, feet, and body. Shortly after this he began to perform miracles. He reportedly healed hundreds of people before he died in 1960.

Above left: *St. Anthony of Padua and the Christ Child,* **painted by Tiepolo. St. Anthony is reported to have traveled out of the body once in order to assist at a service in a church other than the one in which he was physically present at that moment.**

who had appeared at a crucial moment and saved his life.

During World War II an Italian pilot baled out of a blazing plane. His parachute failed to open but he micraculously fell to the ground without injury, and he returned to his base with a strange story to tell. When he had been falling to the ground, a friar had caught him in his arms and carried him gently down to earth. His Commanding Officer said he was obviously suffering from shock, and sent him home on leave. When he told his mother the tale of his escape she said, "That was Padre Pio. I prayed to him so hard for you." Then she showed him a picture of the Padre. "That is the same man!" said the young pilot. He later went to Poggia to thank the padre for his intervention. "That is not the only time I have saved you," said Padre Pio. "At Monastir, when your plane was hit, I made it glide safely to earth." The pilot was astounded because the event the Padre referred to had happened some time before, and there was no normal way he could have known about it.

There are numerous other tales of the amazing bilocations of Padre Pio, a man of our century who, motivated by his vocation as helper and healer, exercised a paranormal faculty whose reality is attested to throughout all ages and cultures of the world. The evidence, taken together, adds up to a substantial case for the reality of the human double—the astral, the etheric, the bioplasmic, the subtle, or the energy body as it has been variously called. It is certainly a strange phenomenon but it has been well attested, and as Don Juan said, "The world is unfathomable. And so are we. . . ."

3

The Projection of the Astral Body

Imagine that you were to wake up from a dream, reach out to switch on a bedside lamp, and find yourself grasping at a void. Coming fully awake, you realize that you are suspended in midair. You are in command of all your sensory faculties, and can see all the familiar features of your room including your own physical body lying peacefully asleep in the bed below. It is difficult for anyone to imagine how he or she would initially react to such an experience. William Gerhardie, the English novelist whose first astral projection occurred in this way, was neither alarmed nor frightened. He said to himself, "Now this *is* something to tell. And

Right: the projection of the astral body as imagined by a modern artist. Nearly all accounts of such experiences include a reference to the cord—usually described as silver in color—that links the astral body to the physical body. People who have researched the subject of astral travel believe that about one person in 100 has had an out-of-the-body experience.

46

"He realized that he could quickly fly anywhere he wished"

Below: British novelist and playwright William Gerhardie, who described his out-of-the-body experience in a semiautobiographical novel, *Resurrection*, published in 1934. After coming back to his body, he checked all the rooms through which he had traveled and was able to verify details he had noticed during his experience.

this is *not* a dream." Gerhardie's account of his first astral projection appears in his partly autobiographical novel *Resurrection*, which was published in 1934. Gerhardie is certain of the authenticity of the experience, and his description is a useful one on which to base an examination of out-of-the-body experiences. The author had no prior knowledge of the phenomenon before it happened to him, and he was able to observe it with the professional writer's curiosity, detachment, and eye for detail. The most convincing evidence for the reality of astral projection for a person who has not experienced it is the fact that many of the same characteristics can be found in accounts from widely different sources. Several of these characteristics are to be found in Gerhardie's narrative.

He remained suspended in the air for several minutes, then felt himself pushed forward and placed on his feet. He staggered to the door but was unable to turn the handle because he had no grip in his hand. He became aware of a strange appendage. At his back was a coil of light that resembled "the strong broad ray of dusty light at the back of a dark cinema projecting onto the screen in front." To Gerhardie's astonishment he found that the cable of light "illumined the face on the pillow, as if attached to the brow of the sleeper. The sleeper was myself, not dead, but breathing peacefully, my mouth slightly open." He saw an aspect of his face he had never seen before, because of course he had never seen himself asleep.

"But I was not dead, I consoled myself; my physical body was sleeping under the blankets, while I was apparently on my feet and as good as before. Yet it wasn't my accustomed self, it was as if my mold was walking through a murky heavy space which, however, gave way easily before my emptiness." While wondering how he would get out, he found himself pushed forward so that either he passed through the door, or the door through him. The apartment was in darkness except for a subdued light that seemed to emanate from his own body. He entered the bathroom and from habit tried to switch on the light, but he found he was unable to press the switch. All the time he was aware of the strange tape of light "like an umbilical cord" between his two bodies, "by means of which the body on the bed was kept breathing while its mold wandered about the flat."

Determined to approach the whole matter scientifically, and to prevent himself from later thinking the whole experience had been a dream, he began to make systematic observations. He noted that the bathroom window was open and the curtain drawn, and he registered the existence of a new towel rack. Passing into other rooms, he noted which windows were closed. He attempted to open the linen closet but failed. Then suddenly he was pushed along "like a half-filled balloon." He flew out through the front door and "hovered in the air, feeling an extraordinary lightness of heart." He realized that he could quickly fly anywhere he wished, but he was afraid that something might happen to sever the link with his sleeping body. His new being, registering his anxiety, flew back to his sleeping body. But, Gerhardie writes, when "I felt it hovering over my old body on the bed, drab disappointment came back to me. 'Not yet,' I said. And again I flew off. When I flew thus swiftly, my consciousness seemed to blot out and only returned when again I walked or moved at a reasonable speed... Consciousness returned suddenly. I was stepping lightly over an open patch of grass . . . The thought occurred to me: how do I know I am not dreaming this? and the answer: look for the lighted cord behind you. It was there, but it was very thin . . . Then, with a jerk that shook me, I opened my eyes. I was in my bedroom . . . Not a detail of my experience had been lost to my mind and there was quite another quality about it all, that of reality, which removed it from the mere memory of a dream . . . I got up, and went through the rooms, checking the mental notes I had made about which windows were closed or open, which curtains drawn; and the evidence in all cases proved correct."

Gerhardie's narrative is a vivid description of what an out-of-the-body experience is like, and its details are corroborated in other accounts. Dr. Robert Crookall, a leading psychic researcher and authority on astral projection, has collected and compared many such accounts in his various books on the subject. Taking Gerhardie as a starting point, it is illuminating to see how many of the features he describes can be paralleled in the description of other astral projectors.

a) Positions of the astral body after separation. Many people report occupying a horizontal position above the physical body for several minutes after separation, and then having a sensation of being pushed into a vertical position.

b) The "strange appendage." The "silver cord" connecting the physical and astral bodies is mentioned in the biblical *Book of Ecclesiastes*, and has been referred to in accounts of OOBEs by people isolated from outside influences—for example by Basuto tribesmen in South Africa. Gerhardie mentions three characteristics of the cord that tally with numerous other accounts: that it is attached to the brow of the physical body (the pineal gland, or "third eye" of occult physiology is in the middle of the brow); that it is luminous; and that it becomes thinner as the distance traveled from the physical body grows greater.

c) The "murky, heavy space." Numerous accounts speak of the conditions first encountered in the astral in terms of fog, grayness, heaviness, or murkiness. Crookall attributes this to consciousness being "enshrouded by the still-unshed body veil." In other words, consciousness is clouded, confused, and unable at first to adjust to the new conditions.

d) Confusion over relation to physical reality. During their first OOBE many people try to do things that they would do in the physical body, such as open doors or closets or move objects, and find they are unable to do so. Many projectors are also surprised to find that they can move at will through walls or doors. The second body feels so real and substantial that it takes time to realize that it has neither the capacities nor the limitations of the physical.

e) An attitude of alert attention. On adjusting to the new conditions, projectors frequently move around and make mental notes of their environment for later corroboration. Many report a sense of enhanced alertness, of sharper mental functioning than they have on the physical plane. They feel more alive, more real. This ability to focus and control attention is one of the charac-

The Psychic Body

"I neither drink nor take drugs, and all I brought to my bed was a considerable nervous exhaustion which sleep was required to restore." So begins William Gerhardie's description of his out-of-the-body experience in his semiautobiographical novel *Resurrection*.

When he became conscious in his astral body he was suspended in mid-air, light as a feather. Once on his feet he felt as if he were defying gravity. In appearance he seemed identical to his physical body on the bed, to which he was attached by a luminous cable.

When he tried to open the door, he found he could not turn the handle. Then he discovered that he could pass right through the door, and he moved around the apartment, making observations, lit by his own cord.

His new body responded to his thoughts and floated this way and that according to his whims. Part of him wished to fly to distant places, but part was afraid this might sever the link with the sleeping body.

When he awoke, he found that his earlier ideas of life after death had been shattered. It seemed to him that we already have a body stored away, rather like a diver's suit, in our own everyday bodies, "always at hand in case of death or for special use."

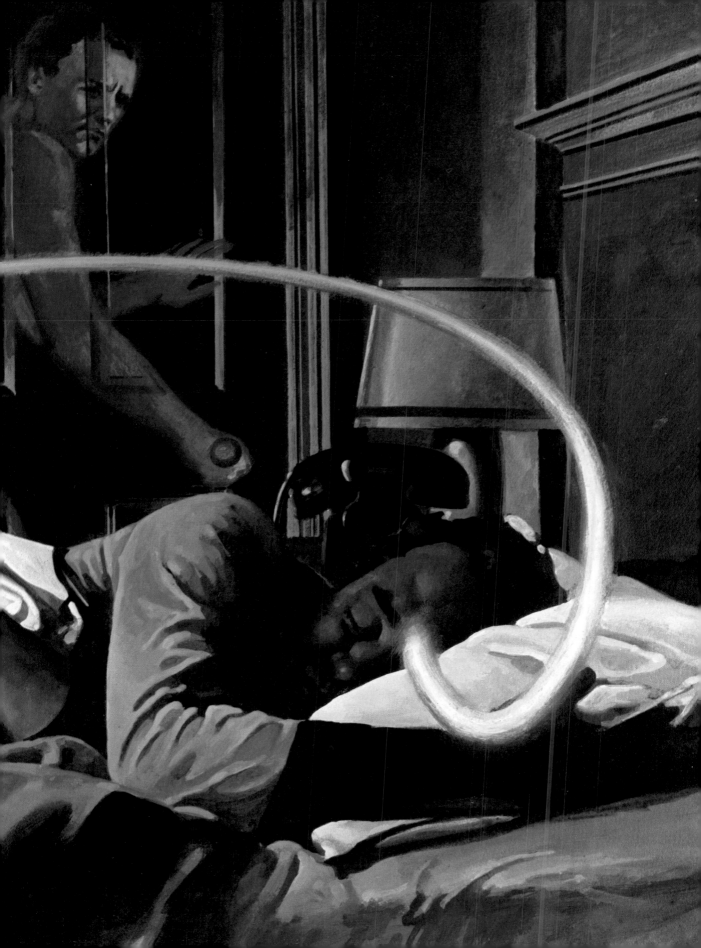

Above: Dr. Robert Crookall, a British scientist who has examined and written about more than 700 cases of astral projection.

teristics of the OOBE that makes it totally undreamlike.
f) Conflicting emotions of exaltation and apprehension. Gerhardie's "extraordinary lightness of heart" when he realized that his subtle body enjoys total freedom of movement is typical. So is his worry lest, possessing such freedom and not knowing the laws that govern this unprecedented experience, he might go too far and sever the link with his physical body.

g) The conscious will as a motor force. Projectors *think* themselves into different locations. Gerhardie realized that he could travel anywhere in the world in a flash simply by willing to do so, and when he thought about his physical self his second body "obeyed and flew back." His observation about the blotting out of consciousness temporarily during high-speed astral travel is confirmed by many other experients.

h) The experience of reentry. Gerhardie speaks of returning to the physical "with a jerk that shook me." The suddenness and shock of the return is an experience reported by many projectors.

Although Gerhardie's account of his first out-of-the-body experience has all the above characteristics in common with the reports of other projectors, it would be misleading to call it a typical case. The list of common characteristics could be considerably extended if we took as points of reference the testi-

Above: an illustration from an old Bible showing the preacher Ecclesiastes reminding the young listener that a day will come when "the silver cord [will] be loosed" and "the spirit shall return unto God who gave it"—an image suggesting release of the astral body.

monies of other experients, but OOBEs come in many varieties and no characteristic, however common, necessarily applies to all of them. The commonest are the presence of the silver cord, the sense of enhanced alertness, and the fact that the conscious will can effect transitions in space in a very short time, though not always instantaneously. Different speeds of travel are reported by different projectors.

It is only in recent years that astral projection has been taken seriously by some psychologists, and there remains a great deal of research work to be done to see whether certain physiological and psychological states precede certain types of astral projection. Crookall has noticed differences between enforced, spontaneous, and deliberate projections, and some experienced projectors offer advice on the most suitable conditions for an out-of-the-body experience. But knowledge, at the present time, remains tentative and incomplete. Apart from the work of Crookall, the only substantial contribution to the subject has been made by Celia Green of the Institute of Psychophysical Research in Oxford, England. She published some of the results of her work in 1968 in a book entitled *Out-of-the-Body Experiences.*

Celia Green's study was based on the testimonies of 326

Below: the ancient and enduring theme of the thread of life is portrayed in this painting of the three Fates. According to mythology, the three women, daughters of Zeus and Themis, determined the destiny of every human. Here Clotho (right) spins the thread of life and Lachesis measures its length, while Atropos waits with some scissors to cut the thread when that span of life is ended.

experients who completed a questionnaire sent out by the Institute. Over 60 percent of the group reported having had only one OOBE, 21 percent had had six or more, and the remaining 18 percent had had between two and five experiences. The group consisted of people of all ages, and showed that the incidence of OOBEs diminished in later life, was common in childhood among subjects who had had more than one experience, and tended to cluster between the ages of 15 and 35 for those who had had only one experience. Most of the cases were not as sustained or full of detailed description as Gerhardie's, but were merely momentary projections. Eighty percent of the subjects reported no awareness of being in a second body, but simply of being a "disembodied consciousness" located at a distance from the physical body. About 32 percent reported that their projections had occurred as a result of an accident or under anesthetic; 12 percent reported them occurring during sleep; 25 percent under conditions of psychological stress; and the rest while awake and active and going about their normal routine.

The very fact that many of the subjects of this study had only one or two fleeting experiences of projection is significant. It suggests that though only a few may undergo prolonged and intense astral journeys, there may be many more who have had some sort of relevant experience at a far less intense level. Two such examples are quoted from the study. The first is a young man who wrote: "During the morning while driving fast along a road the drone of the engine and vibration seemed to lull me into a stupor and I remember I seemed to leave my motorbike like a zoom lens in reverse and was hovering over a hill watching myself and friend tearing along on the road below and I seemed to think "I shouldn't be here, get back on that bike!' and the next instant I was in the saddle again."

The second subject was a waitress who, after working nonstop for 12 hours, left the restaurant to go home and found that she had missed her last bus. She reported:

"However, I started walking as in those days I lived in Jericho, a 15 minute walk at most. I remember feeling so fatigued that I

Left: a drawing from *The Projection of the Astral Body* by Sylvan Muldoon and Hereward Carrington. Muldoon had many experiences of astral projection and described in detail the appearance and apparent function of the astral cord. When the astral body is only slightly separated from the physical body, the cord's diameter is about one and a half inches. As the astral body moves farther away, the cord narrows until it is only as thick as a thread. According to Muldoon, energy passes through the cord from the astral body to the physical body. A heartbeat would be felt in the astral body and the cord at the same moment it was seen in the physical body.

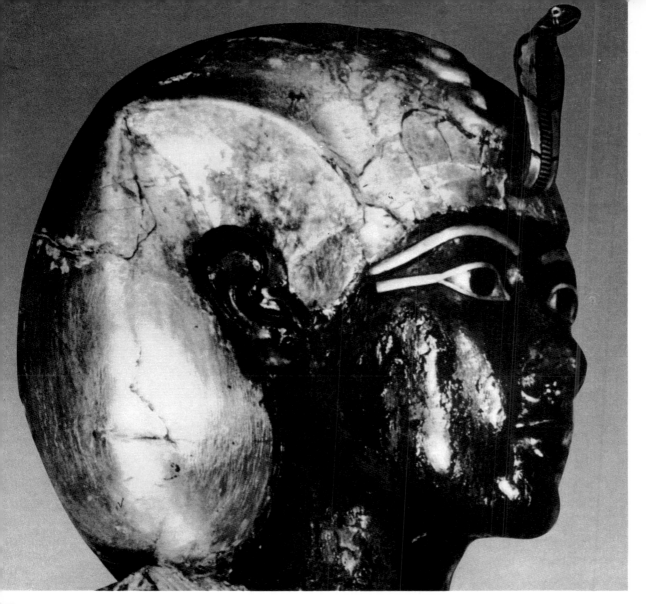

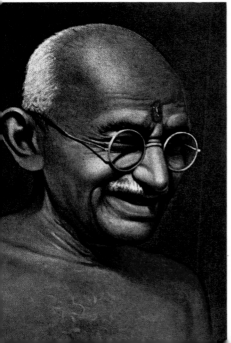

Above: the head of a wooden statue of Tutankhamun, showing the cobra traditionally applied to the foreheads of statues of Egyptian rulers. This symbol of power derives from an ancient legend about how the Egyptian god of creation acquired a third eye, which he placed in the middle of his forehead. Other peoples, such as the Hindus, have also believed in a third and powerful eye.

Left: the late Mahatma Gandhi, like other Hindus before and since his time, wore a caste sign at the point marking the position of the hidden third, or pineal, eye.

wondered if I'd make it and resolved to myself that I'd 'got to keep going' . . . The next I registered, was of hearing the sound of my heels very hollowly and I looked down and watched myself walk round the bend of Beaumont St. into Walton St. I—the bit of me that counts—was up on a level with Worcester College chapel. I saw myself very clearly—it was a summer evening and I was wearing a sleeveless shantung dress. I remember thinking 'so that's how I look to other people.'"

Both of these reports suggest a slightly altered state of consciousness, precipitated in the one case by the monotony and the vibration of the ride, and in the other by fatigue. Neither mentions a sense of possessing a second body, but as Celia Green remarks, many first-time experients are too preoccupied with the novelty of viewing themselves from an objective viewpoint to pay attention to the attributes of their second self. They nevertheless have a total conviction that the second self, even if it is only a "disembodied consciousness" is, as the waitress wrote, "the bit of me that counts."

All systems of occult physiology maintain that the physical and astral bodies are normally completely merged and coincident, but that certain circumstances can throw them out of coincidence. In some people, too, the bonding between the two is looser than normal, and separation can take place relatively easily. The most common cause of separation is a crisis or accident. An experience recounted by the biologist and writer Lyall Watson in his book *The Romeo Error* is typical of this kind of out-of-the-body projection.

The author was driving with a safari group in Kenya when their bus skidded and rolled over several times. He lost consciousness for a moment, and in that time had a brief out-of-the-body experience. He was projected outside the bus and saw that it was about to roll over again, and that when it did one of the occupants would almost certainly be killed. He came around at that point, and took immediate steps to rescue the trapped passenger.

This is a good example of an OOBE serving a useful purpose by enabling a person to obtain information paranormally, act on it and, in Lyall Watson's case, save a life. There are a number of other reported cases of lives being saved as a result of a projection. The most dramatic is that related by a well-known medium, the Reverend Max Hoffman.

At the age of five Hoffman was a victim of a cholera epidemic in Germany. He was diagnosed as dead, and duly buried. The night after his burial his mother woke up to find the child's double standing at her bedside. He told her he was not dead, and begged her to recover his physical body from the grave. He said they would find him lying on his side with his right hand under his right cheek. The apparition returned on three successive nights. Though the father was reluctant to apply to have the grave opened on the dubious evidence of what was probably an anxiety dream, his wife finally prevailed upon him to do so. When the grave was opened the child was found in exactly the position his projected double had told his mother that he was in. Doctors were able to resuscitate him. The physical body had been in a state of suspended animation, just clinging to life, while the astral body went in search of help.

Where the psychic link is strong, as between mother and child or husband and wife, life-saving astral experiences frequently occur. Dr. Crookall has recorded a case of a woman who passed out while taking a bath and lay for some time face down in the water. She left her body and went downstairs to the living room where her husband was reading. She tapped him on the shoulder. He did not actually see her apparition, but he had a sudden compulsion to hurry to the bathroom. He was just in time to drag his wife out of the water and bring her around by artificial respiration. Meanwhile she hovered above the scene, and was later able to describe his every move.

Helping and healing are other useful functions frequently performed by projectors. There is a Scottish doctor who is said to

A Vision of Danger

The biologist and author Lyall Watson was driving with a safari party through the bush of Kenya when suddenly the little bus skidded in the dust and overturned. It rolled over twice and then balanced on the edge of a gully.

A moment later, Watson found himself standing outside the bus looking at it. And yet he could see his own physical body slumped unconscious in the front seat of the bus. A more alarming sight was the head and shoulders of a young boy who had been pushed through the canvas top of the vehicle when it had come to a stop. If the bus fell into the gully—which seemed likely—the boy would be crushed.

The thought scarcely crossed his mind when Watson found himself regaining consciousness in the front of the bus. He rubbed the red dust from his eyes. The memory of what he had just seen was extraordinarily vivid. At once he climbed through the window of the bus and freed the boy, moments before the vehicle rolled over.

Telling the story in his book *The Romeo Error*, published in 1974, Watson said "there is no doubt in my own mind that my vantage point at that moment was detached from my body," but he was unable to provide a scientific explanation for his experience.

project regularly in his second body to give his professional help to people who send out psychic calls at times of distress. One of Crookall's correspondents, a Major Pole, relates how once, when he was desperately ill on a houseboat on the Nile River, the doctor materialized before him, diagnosed his condition, and wrote out a prescription. He chatted meanwhile, as doctors will, telling Major Pole in a matter-of-fact manner about his astral errands of mercy, and mentioning that he always took the precaution of locking his office door when he was projecting so that nobody would disturb his physical body. On returning to England, Major Pole managed to track down his strange benefactor through a radio appeal.

The conviction of the astral voyager that his essential self is not identified with his physical body is an aspect of the experience that can itself be of positive and life-preserving value, for example under conditions of torture or extreme physical hardship. A particularly interesting case of this kind is that of Ed Morrell, a man who had many OOBEs while serving a four-year prison sentence in Arizona some 50 years ago. He later wrote about them in his book *The Twenty-Fifth Man*. Morrell used his secret faculty as a weapon in a psychological war with his guards. The guards were incredibly sadistic in attempting to crush his spirit. They beat him brutally and put him in a tight straightjacket that they doused with water so that it would shrink and increase his pain. During one night of intolerable agony, Morrell suddenly experienced a sense of release from his body. He no longer felt pain, and was joyful and elated by his sense of freedom. He found that

Below: the 19th-century French writer Guy de Maupassant sometimes saw his own double—an experience he seems to have found more annoying than frightening.

Above: Swedish dramatist August Strindberg was prone to emotional illness. Once, while in a state of depression, he involuntarily projected himself to the home of a close relative, who later reported having seen his double.

Below: a painting of the English Romantic poet Percy Bysshe Shelley, who is said to have projected his double on several occasions and to have seen it himself, pointing to the place of his death.

he could pass through the prison walls and travel at will to any place he thought of. Moreover, when he returned to his physical body he felt refreshed and invigorated. The guards redoubled their efforts to break him, once leaving him in the straightjacket for 126 hours, but the astral travels of Morrell's double continued to sustain and revitalize his spirit and his physical body, and nothing they could devise defeated him.

Of course, such a case could be put down to delusion, or explained as a stratagem of the unconscious to overcome the ravages of pain, but Morrell expresses the conviction, typical of the astral traveler, that his essential conscious self, "the bit that counts," had been able to transcend the limitations of time and space. In addition, during his second-body excursions he witnessed events that he was later able to verify, for example a shipwreck, and he saw people unknown to him at the time whom he later met, including his future wife.

Morrell's astral experiences finished after he was released from prison. When he was happy, healthy, and free from stress he found that he could no longer leave his body. This might suggest that out-of-the-body experiences are compensatory and perform the same function as dreams which, according to the psychologist Carl Jung, help to establish a balance in the psyche and make good certain deficiencies in a person's total life experience. Such a theory might account for some astral experiences, but it clearly does not apply to all cases, and it does not imply that the experience is merely subjective. The fact that Morrell and others have acquired information at a distance during out-of-the-body experiences, information that has later been verified and that could not have been obtained through any of the normal channels of sensory communication, stands as clear evidence that in astral experiences the psyche interacts with the objective physical world.

Other theories try to explain out-of-the-body experiences by suggesting that they occur in people suffering from abnormal or pathological conditions such as epilepsy, brain damage, drug addiction, and chronic alcoholism, or during attacks of migraine, influenza, or typhus. Although this may frequently be the case, there are plenty of examples of astral projection by people whose condition can in no way be classed as abnormal or pathological.

In the same way many nervous and unstable people have had psychic experiences. Their instability does not necessarily make these experiences invalid, nor does it account for the hundreds of experiences undergone by people of stable temperaments.

Various famous writers have written about experiences of the double. Guy de Maupassant's double frequently annoyed him when he was writing, and sometimes sat opposite him at his desk and dictated his stories. Shelley, the English romantic poet, frequently projected his double. Once it was seen walking in the woods by Byron and others when the poet was known to be with other friends elsewhere. On another occasion Shelley reported seeing his double himself, pointing toward the sea where he was later to meet his death. The Swedish dramatist Strindberg, a man who lived perilously near the edge of insanity, had moved to Paris after the breakdown of his second marriage. Desperately longing to be back with his family, he had an astral experience in which he found himself in his home and saw his mother-in-law

playing the piano. Soon afterward he received a letter from her saying that she had seen his double appear, and asking if he were ill.

The corroborating testimonies of others, and the fact that verifiable information is sometimes obtained, indicates that though abnormal conditions may facilitate the projection of the double, the double is nevertheless real, and not an hallucination. Some forms of astral projection may arise as psychic compensation, and some may be due to abnormal or pathological conditions, but the phenomenon is so varied and individual that no theory can be all-inclusive. The hale and hearty have out-of-the-body experiences, as well as the ailing and introspective. They can occur spontaneously and for no apparent reason, they can be precipitated by circumstances such as accidents or psychological crises, or they can be deliberately cultivated and induced. Various authors have examined the conditions and methods that are helpful for deliberate astral projections.

Mircea Eliade in *Shamanism* repeatedly makes the point that shamans are "masters of the techniques of ecstasy," and Dr. Robert Crookall has noticed correspondences between these ancient traditional techniques and the descriptions of modern astral projectors. A strange document was obtained by the American psychologist Prescott Hall through a medium who herself had no knowledge of or interest in astral projection. It was published in the *Journal of the American Society for Psychical*

Above: this 15th-century Turkish manuscript illumination shows two shamans dancing to induce a state of ecstasy. Most of the recommended methods of deliberately projecting the astral body are less strenuous, emphasizing techniques of concentration and visualizing.

Right: this Hindu fakir sits in a yoga position, with his tongue pierced by two wooden sticks and his body pierced by small hooks from which fruits are hung, in an effort to free the soul from its earthly nature. Years of practice are required to achieve the difficult physical feats of the yogi and the state of spiritual bliss.

Contacting the Secret Chiefs

According to MacGregor Mathers, one of the founders of the Order of the Golden Dawn, one way he obtained knowledge of magic was through astral projection. In this state he could make contact with the Secret Chiefs, invisible beings who had reached an advanced stage of evolution.

Members of the Order practiced various techniques intended to induce astral visions. The beginner would use the Tattwas, a group of symbols representing the elements. Later, the adept would use more complex symbols—for example, certain Tarot cards, or the I Ching hexagrams.

One of the Golden Dawn "Flying Rolls," or instructional papers, gives a detailed guide to achieving the different degrees of spiritual vision. In the first, Clairvoyance, the adept concentrates on the symbol until he sees it not only with his eyes but with his mind. He articulates certain "Divine Names" connected with the symbol. As the symbol opens and the scene appears, the adept must actively seek objects and persons.

In Astral Projection, the person sends up a "ray" of himself into the scene. Unlike the clairvoyant vision, the scene has a 3-dimensional quality. "If you will," writes the instructor, you will be able to pass through Water, Earth, Air, and Fire. The traveler should converse with forms and persons he meets in this other world and "test them by Divine names and forces."

The third type of spiritual perception is called Rising in the Planes and is a process of formulating a Tree of Life—the Cabala—and then passing upward to the "Great Central Sun of Sacred Power."

Research in 1961, and purported to be detailed instructions on astral projection from a nonphysical source. Looked at together these accounts seem to provide some kind of guideline for the would-be astral projector.

The right weather conditions seem to be important. The air should be clear and dry, the temperature between 70° and 80°F. Conditions of humidity and electrical storms are not favorable. The would-be projector should not eat anything for several hours before an attempt, and should try to avoid a high protein intake for a considerable period before. Favorable physiological conditions are also created by breathing exercises. Heavy rhythmical breathing is said to assist the loosening of the double, and the ancient yogic technique of pranayama, or holding the breath in, is practiced by some projectors to wing the astral body on its way.

Shamans often dance and whirl to the point of exhaustion to induce ecstasy and start the second body on its journey, but less strenuous means are generally recommended for the novice. Relaxation, quiet, deliberate reduction of muscle tension, a mental state of reverie or unfocused consciousness, of withdrawal of attention from the physical world, are essential psychological preconditions. Hall's article also offered a number of images for contemplation in the progressive stages of projection exercises, revealed through the medium's informers. To loosen the astral from the physical body they suggest imagining oneself "as a point in space floating, or as a piece of cloud or as steam." To initiate movement in the astral body they suggest contemplation of the image of a twirling star suspended in space, or images of oneself flying, swinging, or rocking. For the final stage of separation and release of the astral body they gave a number of visualization techniques. For example, they suggest concentrating on the image of a whirlpool or going down through a whirlpool. This gives practice in the exercise of contracting to a point and then expanding. A cone is another image used. The projector must visualize passing through a waterspout or hourglass shape, constructing a cone of circles becoming large or smaller, and turning such a cone inside out. Another exercise is to visualize a tank gradually filling with water, with oneself floating on the top as a point of light. The object is to find a small hole in the side of the tank through which one can pass out.

Robert Monroe, an American businessman who has been having astral experiences regularly for more than 15 years and has learned to control them at will, writes in his book of 1971, *Journeys Out of the Body*: "I believe that anyone can experience existence in a Second Body if the desire is great enough." He also recommends a sequence of exercises to help in astral projection, the key feature of which, as in all methods, is visualization.

But the questions still remain. What is the point of astral projection? What rewards are to be expected from it, and what dangers are incurred? The best way to examine these questions is to consider the accounts of those who are experienced in the techniques of astral projection.

Right: This painting by Columba Krebs, *The Dream of the Double on an Astral Trip*, shows the astral body projecting itself in a spiral path, possibly after concentration on a whirlpool or cone.

The Tattwa cards, representing the
five elements— (left to right) fire,
earth, water, air, and spirit—and
20 subelements formed by combin-
ing them, were used by members of
the Golden Dawn as aids to expanding the consciousness and experiencing visions. The symbols were
derived from Tantra, an Indian
method of using sex as a way of
attaining higher states of consciousness, and were apparently
found by some members of the Gold-
en Dawn in a Theosophical treatise.
To use the Tattwas, one selects
a card and concentrates on its
symbol until no other thought or
image is present in the mind.
The person imagines the symbol as
a kind of door and will it to open.
He then passes through it in his
imagination and experiences a vision. The vision is often related
in some way to the symbol chosen;
for example, if he chooses the
water symbol he may find himself
swimming in a lake or river.

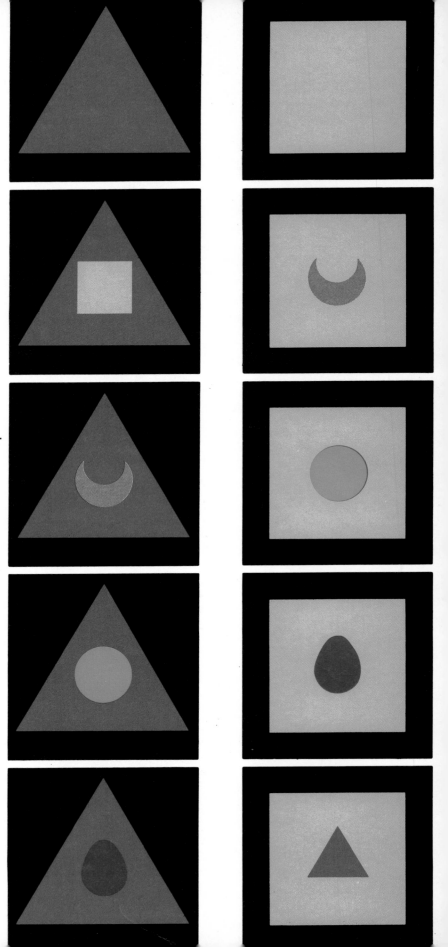

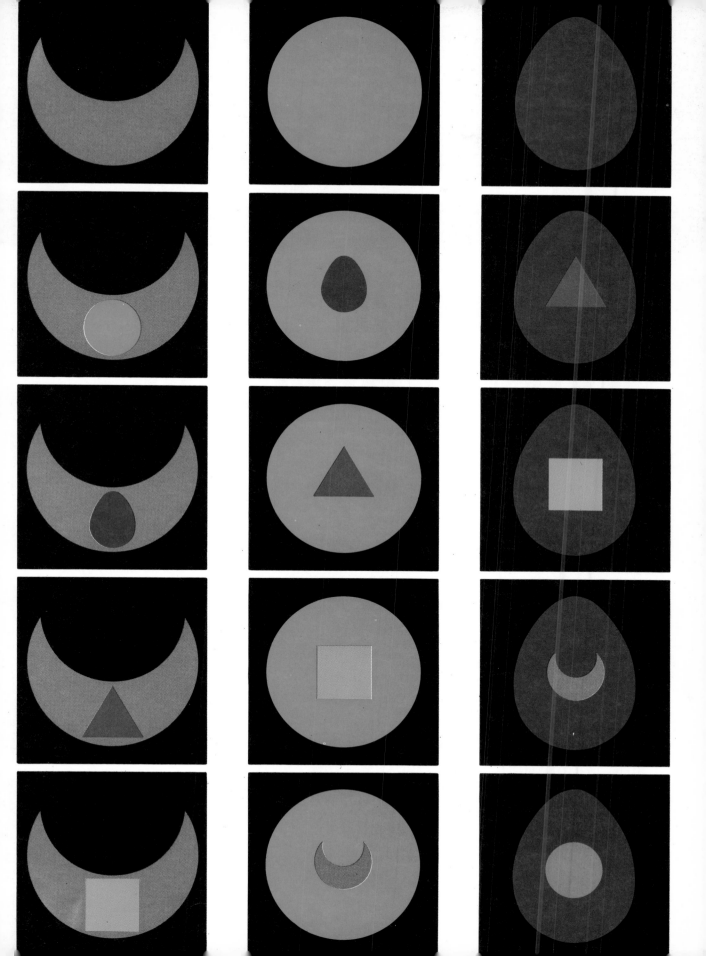

4

Virtuosi of Astral Projection

Sylvan Muldoon had his first experience of spontaneous projection at the age of 12, so when he was 21 and had the experience he later described as "the most unusual I ever had," he was already a seasoned projector. At the time he lived in a small quiet town in Wisconsin. One moonlit summer evening in 1924 he went out for a walk after dinner, and fell into that mood of listlessness, loneliness, and philosophical perplexity that introspective and impressionable young men are prone to. He returned home in disgust, went into his room, locked the door, and flung himself on the bed. When his physical body began to turn numb and his sensory

Right: *Rays of Power*, by psychic artist Columba Krebs, portrays a human being receiving the protective powers emitted by the "Grand Central Sun," which is invisible to ordinary sight. Perhaps significantly, the central beam of light strikes the person in the center of the forehead, the location of the "third eye" and of the projecting silver cord that links the astral body to the physical body when parted.

"He recognized her as the girl he had seen on his astral excursion"

functions deserted him, he recognized the signs of an imminent projection and gave himself over to the experience.

He felt himself rise in the air, then outward and into a vertical position. Gradually the misty atmosphere cleared and he was able to move freely. He walked about indoors for a short time, and then went out into the street. There a bewildering thing happened. He was whipped away at supernormal speed and suddenly found himself in a strange house. There were four people in the room, one of them an attractive girl of about 17, who was sewing a black dress. He found himself propelled without any effort to a position directly in front of the girl, where he remained for a short time watching her. Then he moved around the room, making mental notes of the furniture and various objects. He could see no reason for his being in this place, so he willed himself back to his physical body, taking a last look around before he left and noting from outside that the house was a farmhouse.

Some six weeks later Muldoon was on his way home one afternoon when he saw a girl get out of a car and go into a house. He immediately recognized her as the girl he had seen on his astral excursion, and knowing that she did not live in the house she had entered, he waited for her to come out. When she did he accosted her and asked her bluntly where she lived. The girl said it was none of his business, and would have brushed him off and gone on her way had he not to her amazement started to describe her home, inside and out, in great detail. Muldoon does not record the girl's reaction to his uncanny intelligence, but he states that as a result of this meeting she became a very close friend. He visited her home, which was 15 miles from his own, several times, and recognized all the features and details he had noted on his previous astral visit. He confessed to the girl how he had come by his knowledge, and further convinced her by projecting his visible double into her room. She later participated with him in several experiments.

The thought of disembodied voyeurs hovering around is enough to give any normally modest young women the creeps. Muldoon and Oliver Fox, a British scientist and another experienced projector, are careful to portray themselves as gentlemen of the utmost propriety, both in the body and out of it; but their records are of events of 50 years ago, and in the permissive 1970s it wouldn't be surprising if there were to appear the confessions of a lecherous astral projector. It requires little imagination to conceive how the following experience related by Oliver Fox in his book *Astral Projection* would appear in an updated version.

It was an autumn afternoon in 1913, and Fox lay down in his room "intending to experiment." He was soon able to leave his body and go out into the street. He had walked for about 100 yards when he was "caught up in some strong current and borne away with great velocity." He came to rest in a beautiful small park which he did not recognize. A school party seemed to be in progress, and children dressed in white were playing games and having refreshments under the trees. "Bluish smoke rose from the fires they had lit, and a magnificent amber sunset cast a mellow glow upon the peaceful scene."

Fox walked on till he came to some houses. The front door of one of them was open and he went in, curious to know whether the occupants would become aware of his presence. He mounted a flight of richly carpeted stairs and entered a bedroom on the first landing. "A young lady, dressed in claret-colored velvet, was standing with her back to me, tidying her hair before a mirror. I could see the radiant amber sky through the window by the dressing table, and the girl's rich auburn tresses were gleaming redly in the glamorous light. I noticed that the coverlet of the bed had a crumpled appearance and that there was water in a basin on the washstand. 'Ah, my lady,' I thought, 'you too have been lying down, and now you are making yourself presentable for tea—or is it dinner?' . . ."

Fox moved behind her and stood looking over her shoulder into the mirror. He could see the reflection of her attractive face, but not a trace of his own was visible. Realizing that she could not see him, he wondered whether she would be able to feel him. "I laid a hand upon her shoulder. I distinctly felt the softness of her velvet dress, and then she gave a violent start—so violent that I in my turn was startled too. Instantly my body drew me back and I was awake. . . . The western sky had been blue when I lay down; but on breaking the trance I saw that it was actually the same glorious amber color that it had been in my out-of-the-body experience. . . ."

Both Muldoon's and Fox's narratives could be dismissed as a young man's romantic fantasies if they stood alone, but in the context of the total work of these two men they are perfectly credible descriptions. Muldoon and Fox independently discovered their ability to project, cultivated and developed it, and gradually learned some of the rules governing this strange experience. They were both well aware that the experiences they reported would appear to others to be nothing more than extremely vivid dreams. They wanted to demonstrate that OOBEs were more than dreams, and to encourage others to experiment for themselves and prove the point.

Muldoon's material was written with the encouragement of the distinguished psychical researcher Hereward Carrington. Carrington had published a book, *Modern Psychical Phenomena*, in which he had a chapter on astral projection based on the testimony of a French projector Charles Lancelin. Shortly after its publication he received a letter from Muldoon, who was then unknown to him. Muldoon said that, judging from the material in the book, he doubted whether Lancelin was a conscious projector, and that he could write a book on the things that Lancelin did not know. He gave so many details of his intimate knowledge of the subject in his letter that Carrington eagerly followed up the proposal. Two years later in 1929 their book, *The Projection of the Astral Body*, was published. Most of it was written by Muldoon, and it remains to this day the most informative single work on the subject written by someone who had actually experienced the phenomenon of astral projection.

Carrington makes the point in his Introduction that Muldoon's material is convincing because in fact his claims are modest. He does not profess to have visited distant planets, to have projected into the past, the future, or the spirit world,

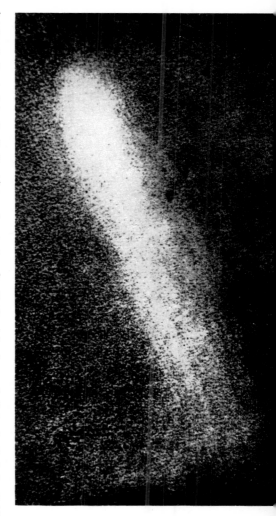

Above: a photograph believed to be that of an astral body swaying, by the French writer on psychic phenomena H. Durville. His book *Phantoms of the Living* tallies in many respects with the discoveries reported by Sylvan Muldoon.

or to have relived his own past incarnations. "He asserts, merely," says Carrington, "that he has been enabled to leave his physical body at will, and travel about in the present, in his immediate vicinity, in some vehicle or other, while fully conscious. This is perfectly rational. . . ." The skeptic may not consider it rational, but it is certainly modest compared with the claims of some other projectors.

Muldoon's first out-of-the-body experience occurred in an environment conducive to the manifestation of paranormal phenomena. His mother was interested in Spiritualism, and one summer she took him and his younger brother to a Spiritualist Association camp in Iowa. They stayed in a rooming house where half a dozen well-known mediums were also staying. In the middle of their first night there the 12-year-old Sylvan awoke after sleeping deeply for several hours. He found himself in a "bewildering stupor," unable either to arouse himself into normal waking consciousness or to fall back to sleep. He couldn't ascertain where he was. He was aware that he was lying somewhere, but when he tried to move he found that he was powerless. He felt as if he were stuck to whatever he was lying on. He was in a condition that he later defined as "astral catalepsy." In medical terms, *catalepsy* is a trancelike condition that sometimes lasts for several weeks. Astral catalepsy, according to Muldoon, is an unpleasant state in which one is fully conscious but completely unable to move.

Other unpleasant sensations followed. He felt that he was floating, that his entire rigid body started vibrating up and down at great speed, and that there was a tremendous pressure at the back of his head which came in spasms. "Amid this pandemonium of bizarre sensations—floating, vibratory, zigzagging, and head-pulling—I began to hear somewhat familiar and seemingly far-distant sounds," he wrote. His senses began to function again, first hearing, then sight. Things seemed hazy at first, then gradually cleared until he saw his surroundings and knew where he was. To his astonishment, however, he found that he was floating toward the ceiling. "It was too unnatural for me to understand, yet too real to deny," he wrote. He had neither experienced nor heard of the existence of the second body at the time, and he assumed that he was in his physical body while mysteriously defying gravity. He was still cataleptic, and remained so for about two minutes after he was "uprighted from the horizontal position to the perpendicular, and placed standing upon the floor of the room."

Suddenly he felt free and able to move. He turned and saw his physical body lying on the bed. An "elastic-like cable" extended between the center of the brow of the physical body and the back of the head of its "astral counterpart." He was swaying from side to side and had difficulty keeping his balance. He was understandably alarmed because he thought that he had died. His first instinct was to go to his mother and awaken her. He went to the door and tried to open it, and was further astonished to find that he just passed through it. He then went around the house trying to shake people and call to them, but his hands passed through them "as though they were but vapors." It was uncanny. All his senses seemed normal except that of touch. He

Above: Hereward Carrington, British psychical researcher, who wrote the introduction to Muldoon's book on astral projection. His early experience as an amateur conjurer was useful in exposing fraudulent mediums.

Right: a drawing from Muldoon's book showing the astral body slightly out of coincidence with the physical body. At the beginning of his first OOBE, Muldoon experienced an unpleasant sensation of floating and vibrating slightly above his physical body while at the same time he felt pressure at the back of his head.

Right: another drawing from the book. The arrows show the path usually taken by the astral body in leaving the physical body. Muldoon claimed that dreams of flying are often caused by the astral body floating in this position, and that the pulling of it back into the physical body will produce a dream of falling.

started to cry. He saw an automobile pass the house and heard the clock strike two. He prowled disconsolately about for 15 minutes, then began to feel a pull on the cable. He became cataleptic again, and was drawn back toward his physical body and into a horizontal position above it. With a shock that shuddered painfully through his entire frame his two bodies came together again and he found himself awake—alive and filled with sensations of awe, amazement, and fear.

The correspondences between Muldoon's and Gerhardie's accounts of their first projections will be obvious. Both found themselves cataleptic and suspended in midair for some time before some force moved them into a standing position. Both were unsteady on their feet at first, but when able to move felt the second body to be substantial enough to attempt to open a door, and were surprised to find that they could pass through doors and walls. Both saw the cable connecting the two bodies and attached to the brow of the physical one, and on returning to the physical both experienced a sudden jerk or shudder. Gerhardie was more adventurous and inquisitive on his first

Left: an illustration from Muldoon's book showing the astral body upright and still within the cord activity range. This is the distance within which the cord will transmit energy from the astral body to the physical one. Activity within the cord ceases when it is stretched to its minimum thickness. Muldoon found that the range of cord activity varied according to his state of health at the time. When he was feeling well it was about 15 feet, but when he was in poor health it was considerably less.

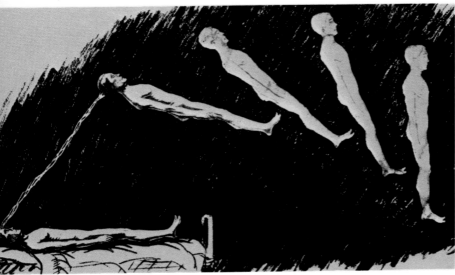

Left: the astral body being pulled back into the physical body, or—to use Muldoon's term—*interiorizing*. He claimed that there are three types of interiorization: the spiral fall and straight fall, both of which accompany a dream of falling and are unpleasant sensations, and the slow vibratory fall, the normal method, which is gentle and controlled.

excursion, and learned more about the potentials of distant projection, but Muldoon was only 12 years old and his reaction of fear, loneliness, and anxiety to contact other people is only to be expected.

When he became accustomed to the experience of astral projection, Muldoon began to investigate the phenomenon in a systematic way and to develop his own theories about it. He came to the conclusion that prolonged projection from a state of sleep, such as he had experienced the first time, was probably rare, but that "instantaneous projection" was not uncommon and might happen to people without their realizing it. He wrote: "When something unusual or unnatural occurs to upset the harmony of the physical—a shock, a jolt, a broken habit, an intense unappeased desire, sickness—in fact, anything which would cause a lack of perfect material coordination—there is always a jar to the astral." Even so commonplace an event as the jolt a person experiences when he descends a staircase in the dark and, at the bottom, tries to take an extra step, can momentarily jar the astral body out of coincidence with the

Right: this self-portrait by the student of magic Austin Spare shows the artist in what he called the death posture, bent slightly forward, his fingers blocking his nostrils and starving the lungs of oxygen. He is surrounded by creatures of the unconscious and symbols of magic. Under the guidance of a woman named Mrs. Paterson, who practiced witchcraft, Spare claimed to have visited places outside terrestrial reality—"spaces outside space"—into which he would be suddenly precipitated. His paintings and drawings reflect his visions of and voyages into the psychic world.

Above: this old engraving shows the astral form floating upward from the body of a sleeping girl. According to Muldoon, the most pleasant way to promote astral projection is to construct a dream that involves an upward motion such as flying and to dwell on this just before falling asleep.

Right: a painting of *The Prophet Muhammad's Night Journey* showing Muhammad traveling through the seven celestial spheres to approach God. Several people who have experienced astral travel have reported the existence of more than one plane of reality. The French psychic Yram claimed that humans have several bodies, of varying degrees of density, capable of passing through materials of certain densities. Robert Monroe, an American who has written about and experienced OOBEs, believes that there are three planes of reality: Locales I, II, and III. The first is the physical world of ordinary consciousness; the second is the plane of thought; and the third, Localle III, is both physical and mental.

physical. In sleep, Muldoon maintained, the astral body always moves slightly out of coincidence, perhaps only a fraction of an inch, but often much more. "If you could hold consciousness up to the very last moment, in the hypnagogic state," Muldoon says, "you could feel this act of discoincidence, as indeed nervous and fatigued people often do."

Muldoon's theory of the purpose of what he calls discoincidence during sleep is interesting, particularly in the light of modern Soviet research into the "energy body" through means of electrophotography. The astral body, he claims, is a "condenser" of cosmic energy, and it regularly discoincides from the physical in order to become recharged with energy. So in the person who is fatigued or run down discoincidence will be more pronounced, and will occur more frequently than in people of more robust constitution. This theory has a certain logic and appeal, for it would explain the fact that people who have OOBEs are often frail. Muldoon himself was of delicate health throughout his life. Eliade remarks that shamans are usually recruited from among the delicate and sickly, and a true shaman is "a sick man who has succeeded in curing himself." It would also explain the fact that many projectors, for example Ed Morrell, report that they return from their astral travels feeling refreshed and revitalized.

"If you ask me which is the most pleasant way to promote astral projection," Muldoon wrote, "I should answer by saying 'dream control.'" The astral body may be called the "dream body," he said, "for it is in that body that we dream—even though we may be in coincidence or completely separated from the physical." The first stage of the dream control method of promoting projection involves holding consciousness up to the very moment of falling asleep, or as Muldoon calls it, "rising to sleep." To do this he recommends holding an arm in the air so that it will begin to sway and tend to fall when sleep comes, resulting in a slight awakening. The next stage is to construct an appropriate dream, to dwell on it and hold it clearly in mind so that it continues when the body completely succumbs to sleep. The dream should be one that involves an upward and outward movement of the body, a dream of flying or of going up in an elevator, for example. Muldoon claims that "a properly constructed dream is sure to move the astral body out," and explains that "the astral naturally moves out of coincidence at the

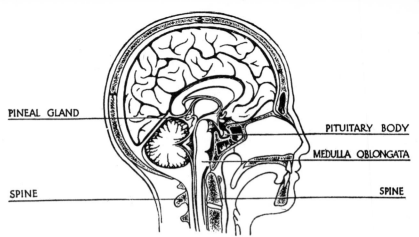

PINEAL GLAND

PITUITARY BODY

MEDULLA OBLONGATA

SPINE

SPINE

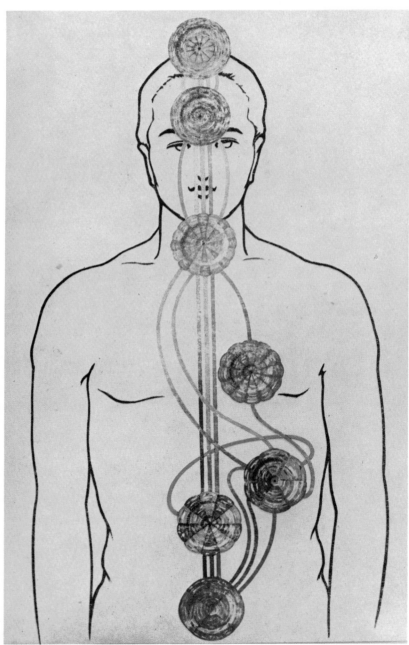

Above: a diagram of the head taken from C. W. Leadbeater's book *The Chakras* showing the pineal gland, located slightly behind the pituitary. Science has not discovered the function, if any, of this gland; many psychics believe it may be the doorway through which the astral body is released. Oliver Fox observed that he felt a distinct click in this part of the head on returning from a "dream of knowledge."

Left: another illustration from Leadbeater's book—this one entitled *The Streams of Vitality*. It shows the locations of the seven chakras and the paths along which energy flows from one to another.

Right: the *Brow Chakra*, an illustration from Leadbeater's book. This chakra is believed to be the center of psychic visions and, when fully developed, to endow the person with clairvoyance. According to Leadbeater the chakras can actually be seen by "a fairly evolved and intelligent person" who has brought his own chakras "to some extent into working order."

moment of sleep; it naturally starts itself, and that is just the moment when you must mentally project yourself into the up-going elevator (or whatever the dream may be) and 'keep going.' . . . In such a dream the astral body acts out exactly whatever the dream may be. . . . If you become *completely* conscious in such a dream, you would usually find yourself in some place corresponding to the place of action which was last seen in the dream."

Oliver Fox also maintained the reality of the dream world and the possibility of projecting the astral body by means of dream control. His own research, he wrote, began with a dream.

"I dreamed that I was standing on the pavement outside my home. The sun was rising behind the Roman wall, and the waters

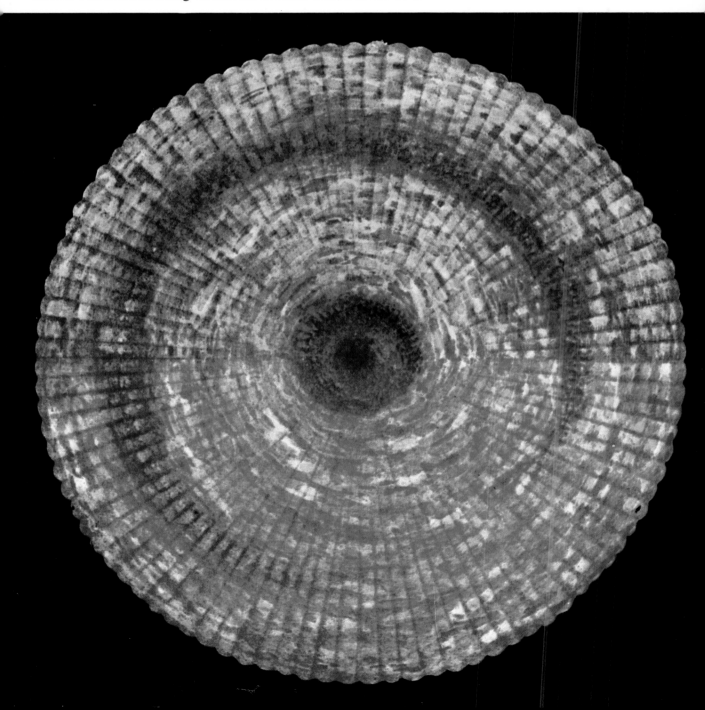

These four drawings from *The Secret of the Golden Flower*, a Chinese "Book of Life," show (above, below, and opposite) four stages of meditation, in which the person transforms himself and releases his primal spirit.
Above: *Gathering the Light*. This phrase is reminiscent of Fox's gathering up and compressing the "incorporeal self," which could then be astrally projected.
Below: *Origin of a New Being in the Place of Power*. Only by following specific instructions as to posture, breathing, and concentration can the person develop within him the immortal spirit body.

of Bletchingden Bay were sparkling in the morning light. I could see the tall trees at the corner of the road and the top of the old gray tower beyond the Forty Steps. . . . Now the pavement was not of the ordinary type, but consisted of small, bluish-gray rectangular stones, with their long sides at right-angles to the white kerb. I was about to enter the house when, on glancing casually at these stones, my attention became riveted by a passing strange phenomenon so extraordinary that I could not believe my eyes—they had seemingly all changed their position in the night, and the long sides were now parallel to the kerb! Then the solution flashed upon me: though this glorious summer morning seemed as real as could be, I was *dreaming*."

Fox called the kind of dream in which one is conscious of dreaming a "Dream of Knowledge," and he discovered that with practice he could prolong and control such dreams. He also found that in a Dream of Knowledge he could do some curious things. "I could glide along the surface of the ground, passing through seemingly solid walls, etc., at a great speed, or I could levitate to a height of about 100 feet and then glide. . . . I could also do some intriguing little tricks at will, such as moving objects without visible contact, and molding the plastic matter into new forms." He found that the effort of prolonging a Dream of Knowledge produced a pain in the head, which he realized was a warning "to resist no longer the call of my body." As the call of the body grew stronger he experienced a period of dual consciousness, in which he could simultaneously feel himself standing in his dream body and lying on his bed, and see both the dream scenery and his bedroom.

What, he wondered, would happen if he tried to resist the call back to the body and disregarded the pain in his head? He screwed up his courage to make the experiment, and had "a never-to-be-forgotten adventure."

He dreamed that he was walking beside the sea. "It was morning; the sky a light blue; the foam-flecked waves were greenish in the sunshine." He became aware that he was dreaming, and when he felt the pull back to the body he exerted his will to continue in the dream. "A battle ensued; now my bedroom became clearly visible and the shore-line brighter." The pain in his head became increasingly intense and he fought against it, resolutely willing to remain in the dream world. Then suddenly the pain ceased, something seemed to go click in his brain, and he felt delightfully free. He continued his walk, "reveling in the beauty of the morning. . . . It seemed to me that the apparently solid shore and sunlit waves were not the physical land and sea; that my body was lying in bed, half a mile away at Forest View; but I could not feel the *truth* of this. I seemed to be completely severed from that physical body. At this point I became aware of a man and boy approaching. As they passed me they were talking together; they did not seem to see me, but I was not quite sure. A little later, however, when I met another man and asked him the time, he took no notice and was evidently unaware of my presence."

He began to get worried. When he willed to end the dream and wake up nothing happened. He didn't know how much time had elapsed in the physical world. He wondered whether he was dead, and then began to worry lest, if he were alive, he should be prematurely buried. He desperately willed to get back to the physical, but the shore-scene remained vividly before him. He tried to hold down a mounting feeling of panic. He willed and willed, and suddenly something seemed to snap, he felt another click in his brain, and he found that he was awake and in his bedroom—but he was completely paralyzed. After some time he managed to move a little finger, then other fingers, then his hand, and at last he emerged with relief from his state of catalepsy.

Fox attributed the click in the head to the passage of the astral body through what he called the "pineal door." He later found that he could go into a trance state and induce projection by concentrating on the pineal gland and willing to ascend through it. He imagined the process as one of gathering up and compressing the "incorporeal self," rushing it to a point in the pineal gland, and hurling it against a kind of trap door that would briefly be forced open and then click shut after the astral body had passed through. He stressed, however, that though this was what he felt happened in projection, his readers were at liberty to take it as a figurative description.

Fox tended to experience more adventurous and far-flung projections than Muldoon. Once he found himself in an oriental city and saw street bazaars and a huge black sculptured elephant in a kneeling position. On another terrifying occasion he was bound, bleeding and naked, to an X-shaped framework and saw robed figures moving about in the dimness. He roamed through an astral counterpart of London where among all the familiar features there were buildings and monuments that he did not recognize and thought must belong to the past or future of the city. Sometimes he practiced *skrying*, which he described as "like gliding, but in a vertical direction," or as "rising through the planes."

The idea of the existence of several planes or dimensions of the astral world was central in the conceptual scheme of Yram, a mysterious French contemporary of Fox, whose true identity remains unknown. The English version of his book was published in 1900 under the title *Practical Astral Projection*. Yram believed that humans have not merely two but several bodies, and that "as the conscious will penetrates into new dimensions it uses a corresponding body." The bodies were of different degrees of density, and Yram sometimes experienced difficulty in passing through walls when he was "using a double of too material a quality." At other times he could pass through them as if they were not there at all because, he said, he had "exteriorized a less material double." His travels were as dramatic as Fox's, and they took him to several parts of the material world as well as through the several planes of the astral. On the lower planes he sometimes was attacked by "rather unpleasant entities," and once he was hardly out of his body when he "received a terrific slap in the face without being able to find whence it came."

To compensate for such unpleasant experiences, Yram sometimes projected to higher spiritual planes where the beings he met and the visions he had were of great beauty and religious intensity. On one stratum he would meet and chat with deceased

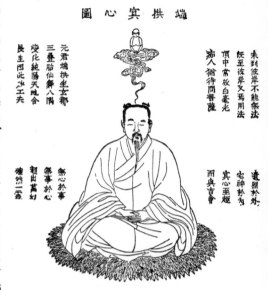

Above: *Separation of the Spirit Body for Independent Existence.* The book further describes the experience as follows: "The heavenly heart rises to the summit of the Creative, where it expands in complete freedom . . . body and heart must be left completely released. All entanglements have disappeared without trace."

Below: the final stage of meditation, *The Center in the Midst of the Conditions*, in which the spirit body has been fully liberated.

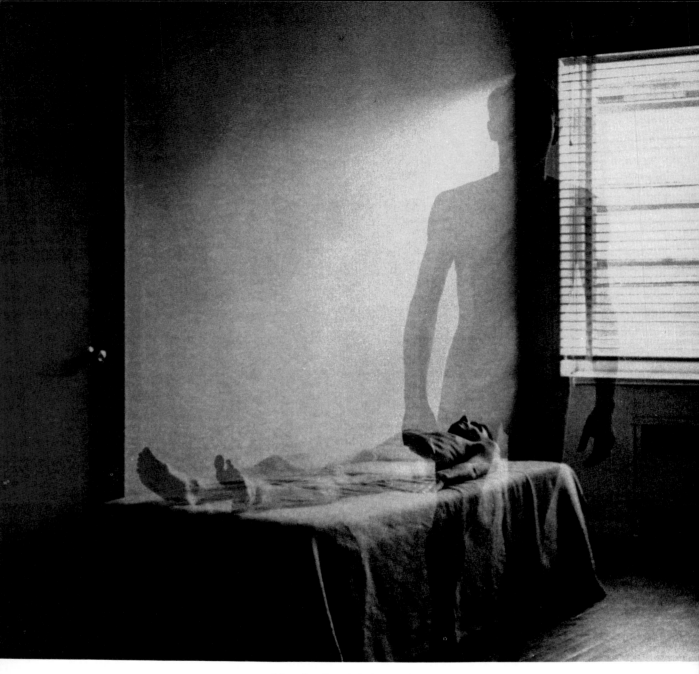

friends. Explaining this he wrote: "In order to appreciate this
properly you must remember that I am not telling you a dream,
not a vision, I am telling you of a real fact, a conscious act
accomplished with an absolutely clear mind, with perfect
freedom, and without any trace of sleep. You are there near
your friends, talking affectionately, fully conscious of your
double state, which you can terminate immediately whenever
you wish. As all your psychical elements are active, a thought is
all that is needed to bring you straight back to your body with a
lucidity equal to that of any moment of the day."

Yram's writing style tends to be as ethereal and lacking substance as his double, and of all the virtuosi of astral projection,
his approach is the least critical and scientific. His narrative
would not convince any skeptic that his experiences were any-

This photomontage was taken for Robert Monroe's book *Journeys Out of the Body*, in which he describes his astral travels.

thing more than vivid dreams or nightmares, though anyone familiar with the literature of projection will recognize in it elements that suggest that at least some of his OOBEs were authentic. At the opposite extreme is Robert Monroe who, as a result of having had many OOBEs, established a Mind Research Institute in Virginia. His book is the most level-headed and analytical of all experients' records.

Monroe recalls two out-of-body experiences from his childhood, one of which involved an apparent projection 30 years into the future and a foresight of television before it was invented. But it was not until much later in life that he began to have OOBEs regularly. It started alarmingly. On several occasions when he lay down he suffered a severe and inexplicable abdominal cramp. Then his entire body began vibrating. The condition lasted for some time, then ceased abruptly. Monroe consulted a physician and a psychologist, but neither could offer any explanation of the experience. He got accustomed to simply waiting patiently for the pain and the vibrations to pass. One evening as the pain occurred, he happened to let his arm fall loosely over the side of the bed. His fingers were resting on the bedside rug, but when he moved them slightly they seemed to pass through the rug to the floor beneath, and when he pushed they seemed to penetrate the floor as well. Curious, he pushed deeper until his entire arm was through the floor and his hand through the ceiling of the room below. He was sure that he was fully awake, and made careful mental notes of the familiar features of his room and the moonlit landscape through the window, but the sensation persisted. His fingers splashed about in a pool of water. When the vibrations began to abate he snatched his arm back onto the bed for fear that the floor might close and sever it.

Some four weeks after this incident, Monroe again experienced the vibrations, and while he was waiting for them to pass he "just happened to think how nice it would be to take a glider up and fly the next afternoon." Soon after this he felt something pressing against his shoulder and back, and thought at first that he had fallen out of bed and was leaning against a wall. Then he realized that it was not the wall but the ceiling. He was floating against it like a balloon, and down below he could see his wife in bed with someone. When he looked closer and saw that the other person was himself, his first thought was that he had died, but when in a panic he tried to get back into his physical body, he found that he had no difficulty in doing so.

This experience started Monroe on a long program of research. In his book he reports several experiments undertaken with the cooperation of other people in which he projected his second body to a distant location and returned with correct information about what those people were doing at the time. Once he projected to visit a woman friend who was on vacation somewhere on the New Jersey coast. He didn't know exactly where she was, and she was not aware that he was going to attempt an experiment. About three o'clock on a Saturday afternoon he lay down and employed one of the techniques he had developed to separate his second body, at the same time willing it to visit his friend wherever she was. He saw a scene in what appeared to be a kitchen. His friend and two teenage girls were sitting there chatting. They held glasses in their hands. He remained a while, and then decided to try something he had never attempted before. He went over to the woman and pinched her just below her ribcage. He was somewhat surprised when she let out a loud "Ow!" Well, he thought, he had given her something to remember the occasion by, and he waited impatiently for Monday, when they would meet again at work. Asked what she had been doing between three and four on Saturday, the woman answered after some thought that she had been sitting in the kitchen of a beach cottage with her niece and her niece's friend. They had been doing nothing in particular, she said, mostly talking and drinking cola. Monroe had to prompt her to remember the pinch, but when he mentioned it she asked in amazement, "Was that you?" She showed him two bruise marks on her side at exactly the spot where he had pinched her.

Monroe does not use the term "astral" when he writes about his OOBEs, but he firmly believes he has visited different planes of reality that he calls "Locales I, II, and III." Locale I is the here-and-now physical world. Locale II is a "thought world" and is "the *natural* environment of the Second Body." Locale III, Monroe writes, "seems to interpenetrate our physical world, yet spans limitless reaches beyond comprehension." In it "reality is composed of deepest desires and most frantic fears. Thought is action . . . it is the well-spring of existence . . . the vital creative force that produces energy, assembles 'matter' into form, and provides channels of perception and communication." What we call heaven and hell are located in Locale II, which is inhabited by various entities and creatures that are really "thought forms."

Monroe states that on visits to Locale II he has met the dead, and he believes that "human personality survives the transition of death and continues in Locale II." Locale III is a physical and material world weirdly like, but at the same time in many details unlike, the world we know. There is a natural environment similar to the Earth's. There are people, cities, roads, businesses, all the signs of a civilization. But it is a civilization based on different technologies and with different customs. There are no electrical devices, no signs of the use of oil or the principle of internal combustion as power sources. Scientific development is apparently less advanced than on Earth, but Locale III cannot be a period of our past history because our science was never at the Locale III stage. On visits there, Monroe has inhabited a different body and lived a different life from his earthly one.

When Monroe writes about his experiences in Locale III he strains his readers' credulity to the utmost. It is interesting, though, and perhaps relevant to note that since 1971 when his book was first published, theoretical physicists working in the field of advanced quantum mechanics have come up with the hypothesis that there exist multiple Universes, all basically similar but with slight differences, and that "transition events" — which could take the form of OOBEs — between these Universes can and do occur. In fact, in the light of these recent developments in theoretical physics, even the convinced skeptic should hesitate before dismissing accounts of astral projection as nothing more than mere fantasy.

5

Beyond the Veil

There are a number of reported instances of false deaths which seem to suggest that the second body may survive the death of the physical body, at least for a time. One of the most famous and bizarre is the case of the Reverend Bertrand, a Huguenot clergyman. Both Richard Hodgson and William James, two of the most serious 19th-century psychical researchers, heard his narrative at first hand, checked it, and were convinced of its authenticity. The case was reported in the *Proceedings for the Society for Psychical Research* in 1892. While climbing in the Alps with a party of students and an old guide, the Reverend Bertrand felt weary. He decided to

Right: this painting, *Is this not Great Babylon that I have built?*, is by the Irish poet and painter G. W. Russell, better known as A.E. The soul was a recurring theme in A.E.'s work. In this painting it is shown ascending from the physical body. Inclined to mysticism, A.E. was attracted to the teachings of Theosophy and to those of the great Indian mystics.

"Suddenly he had a sensation of being irres- istibly pulled downward"

rest while the others went up to the summit, which he had in any case visited several times before. He instructed the guide to take the party up by a path to the left and to come down by the right. When they had gone he sat down to rest with his legs dangling over a precipice. After a time he put a cigar in his mouth and struck a match to light it, but suddenly a curious feeling came over him. He watched the match burn his fingers, but he couldn't throw it down, nor could he move his limbs. Realizing that he was freezing to death, he began to pray; then, giving up hope of survival, he decided to study the process of dying.

He remained conscious while the icy paralysis progressively gripped all his bodily functions, then he felt his head become unbearably cold and suddenly had the sensation of separating from his physical body. He could see it below him, "deadly pale, with a yellowish-blue color, holding a cigar in its mouth and a match in its two burned fingers," and he felt that he was "a captive balloon still attached to Earth by a kind of elastic string and going up, always up." He felt exultant and alive and only wished that he could cut the thread that still connected him with the physical. He could see the party continuing their climb, and noted that the guide had disregarded his instructions and gone up by the right instead of the left. He also watched the guide steal a leg of chicken and some drinks from his bottle of Madeira, and he thought, "Go on, old fellow, eat the whole chicken if you choose, for I hope my miserable corpse will never eat or drink again."

Traveling further in his astral body, he saw his wife, who was due to join him in Lucerne the following day, descend from a carriage with four other people and go into a hotel at Lungren. But his only emotion was regret that "the thread, though thinner than ever, was not cut."

Suddenly he had a sensation of being irresistibly pulled downward. The party had returned to where they had left him, and the guide was rubbing his body to restore circulation. He felt that he was a balloon being hauled down to earth. His description of his reentry into the physical body emphasizes the violence of the experience, which numerous other projectors have noted: "When I reached my body again I had a last hope—the balloon seemed much too big for the mouth. Suddenly I uttered an awful roar, like a wild beast; the corpse swallowed the balloon, and Bertrand was Bertrand again."

The old guide might reasonably have expected the revived clergyman to be grateful to him for saving his life, so he was astounded when Bertrand admonished him for disobeying his instructions as to the route and for stealing some of his Madeira and the chicken leg. When the party returned to Lucerne, Bertrand astonished his wife by asking whether there had been five people in the carriage and if they had stopped *en route* at the hotel in Lungren.

"Yes," she said, "But who told you?"

A more modern case of false death is that of Private George Ritchie, who on December 20, 1943, was brought back to life with an injection of adrenalin directly into the heart after being officially dead for nine minutes. The army doctor who had signed the death certificate pronounced the case "the most baffling circumstance of his career," and both he and a nurse signed affidavits attesting that Private Ritchie had died. But during those nine minutes of not being alive the young soldier had a sequence of experiences that he remained grateful for ever afterward. Now a psychiatrist in Charlottesville, Virginia, Dr. Ritchie believes that he was allowed to return to this life "so that I could learn about man and then serve God." He described his strange experience in *Guideposts* magazine in 1963.

Having just completed basic training, Ritchie was given the "unheard-of break for a private" of being assigned to the Army medical school at Richmond, Virginia, but on the day he was due to go there he developed what at first was a chest cold. He tried to combat it with aspirin, but his condition rapidly got worse, he developed a high fever, and finally he lost consciousness. He surfaced slightly with blurred impressions of traveling in an ambulance and of struggling to get to his feet to have an X-ray taken. Then everything went blank until he suddenly woke up to find himself lying in a dimly lit, unfamiliar room. His first thought was that he would miss the train to Richmond, and he sprang out of bed to look for his uniform. It was nowhere to be seen, but when he turned back to the bed he had just left he saw that someone was lying on it. The man was obviously dead. "The slack jaw, the gray skin, were awful," he said. When he looked closer he saw on the left hand of the corpse his own fraternity ring from his college days, which he had worn for two years.

He fled from the room, his only thought being that he must get to Richmond. In the hall an orderly seemed to walk right through him without seeing him. What if the people at the medical school couldn't see him either? he thought as he sped through the dark night toward Richmond. He didn't know whether he was running or flying but he was aware of the landscape slipping by. Then he stopped his headlong flight to take stock of his situation. He was standing by a telephone pole in a town by a large river. He tried to touch the guy wire, but his hand passed right through it. "In some unimaginable way," he later wrote, "I had lost my firmness of flesh, the hand that could grip that wire, the body that other people saw." Realizing that he wasn't going to be able to pursue his medical career in his present nonphysical form, he decided that he must get back and rejoin his physical body as fast as he could.

He had no trouble returning to the hospital. He was there as soon as he thought of it. But the problem was to find his body. He rushed from ward to ward and room to room, scrutinizing the faces of sleeping soldiers, and several times he thought he recognized himself but found that the fraternity ring was lacking. Then he found the ring on the left hand of a figure covered with a sheet. For the first time, the thought occurred to him that, "This is death. *This* is what we human beings call 'death,' this splitting up of one's self."

Then he had a religious illumination. The room filled with light and he felt the presence of God, and simultaneously his whole life, "every event and thought and conversation, as palpable as a series of pictures," passed before him in review. Suddenly he was in another world, or a world coextensive with

Above: the psychologist, philosopher, and psychical researcher William James. He investigated an out-of-the-body experience undergone by a clergyman, the Rev. J. L. Bertrand, while mountain-climbing.

Above: psychic Alex Tanous photographed during an ASPR experiment in out-of-the-body vision.

Above right: the rotatable disk of the optical image device used in OOB experiments at the ASPR. One of five images, randomly selected, is flashed onto one of the quadrants, also randomly selected, and the image revealed through a window in the device itself. Because there is a choice of images, all of which could theoretically be seen by clairvoyance, frequent on-target responses would suggest that the subject was viewing the machine, with the chosen image displayed, rather than seeing all the images clairvoyantly.

Above: Dr. Charles T. Tart, an American psychologist and para-psychologist, at the controls of an ESP teaching machine. Dr. Tart has done considerable research on out-of-the-body experiences, including those of Robert Monroe. Today scientists in laboratories all over the world are seriously investigating psychic experiences.

and "strangely superimposed on our familiar world." It was a world thronged with unhappy and desperate looking people, all trying vainly to make contact with others. He surmised that they were the dead, still preoccupied with earthly cares, as he had been in trying to get to Richmond. He wondered if this was hell. "To care most when you are most powerless; this would be hell indeed," he said.

He went on to visit two other worlds—not, he said, so-called spirit worlds, "for they were too real, too solid." He realized they were also worlds that had been there all along, but could only be seen with "a new openness of wisdom." The first of these was a world of philosophers and artists of all kinds, men concerned not "with earthly things, but . . . with truth," and in it

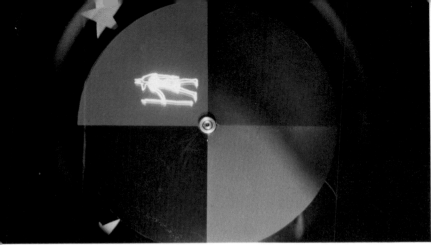

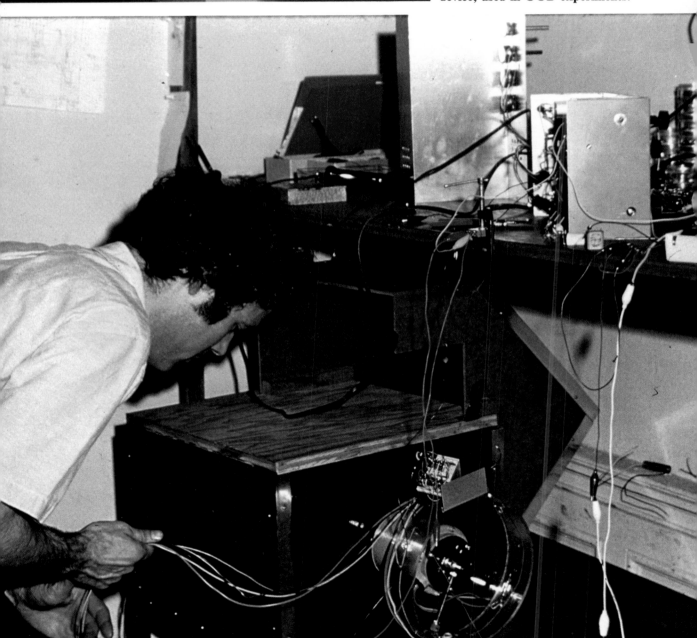

Below: an ASPR staff physicist working with the optical image device, used in OOB experiments.

Above: Auckland Campbell Geddes, a British physician and professor of anatomy who described, in a paper read to the Royal Medical Society, an out-of-the-body experience undergone by a person who was critically ill.

Right: four images of the "astral bodies" of different people in different physical and mental states, from C. W. Leadbeater's book *Man Visible and Invisible*. The first picture at right purports to show the astral body of the "savage," which consists largely of red, symbolizing sensuality. The second picture shows that of the "miser," the horizontal lines indicating a person who has "shut himself away from the world." The third picture, "the average man in love," is more or less self-explanatory; and the fourth, "the developed man," shows the strong yellow light signifying intellect.

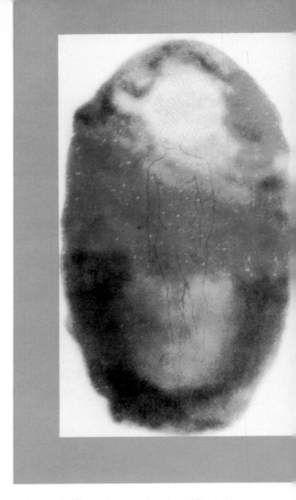

there were universities and great libraries and scientific laboratories. He only had a glimpse of the final world, one far away from earth and out of all relation to it, where the buildings and the people were all blindingly bright. "At that time," he wrote, "I had not read the *Book of Revelation*, nor, incidentally, anything on the subject of life after death."

Then he woke up in his physical body. To the astonishment of the onlookers—the doctor, the nurse, and the orderly who had been assigned to prepare him for the morgue and who had noticed feeble signs of life in the corpse—he showed no symptoms of brain damage although he had not drawn breath for the full nine minutes of his excursion into the beyond.

In modern Western societies the accredited method of seeking truth has tended to be the scientific method, and it is an axiom of science that no statement can qualify as truth unless there are tests it can be subjected to. The trouble with the survival-of-death and the second-body hypotheses is that the evidence supporting them is based on subjective reports such as those of Bertrand and Ritchie. Because there are no tests that scientists can set up to prove or disprove the theories, they have tended to ignore the problems. But in recent years there has been a growing dissatisfaction among young scientists with the demarcations of the traditional scientific approach. Charles T. Tart, Professor of Psychology at the University of California, has pinpointed its limitations for the scientifically curious.

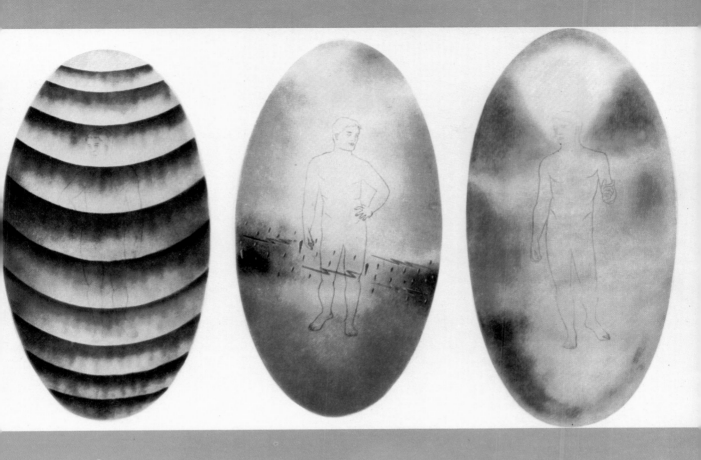

Tart argues that Western science has been a science dealing with one state of consciousness only. Because of this it only has access to a limited area of reality and a limited range of truths. He wants to extend the range of scientific inquiry to deal with other levels of consciousness. One way to do this would be to encourage groups of highly skilled practitioners to attain certain states of consciousness and to discuss and compare their findings. Till that time, however, we will have to depend for our knowledge on those recorded accounts which seem to be genuine. Two such accounts are vouched for by doctors, and both appear to be reliable.

Addressing the Royal Medical Society of Edinburgh in 1937, Sir Auckland (later Lord) Geddes, a distinguished professor of anatomy, read his colleagues a description of an OOBE that he said had been given to him by another physician who wished to remain anonymous. The experience, in fact, was probably his own, but he no doubt felt that to present it as such at that time would be to jeopardize his professional reputation.

On November 9, a few minutes after midnight, the physician in question began to feel very ill. His condition worsened in the night, and by morning he realized that his state was critical. He was unable even to ring for assistance, however, and he "quite placidly gave up the attempt." Suddenly he realized that he was separating into two distinct types of consciousness, an "A consciousness" connected with his ego, and a "B consciousness"

Right: the writer Ernest Hemingway, who had an out-of-the-body experience in 1918 while fighting in World War I in Italy. He had been hit in the leg by shrapnel. As he lay in the trench he suddenly felt as if "my soul or something was coming right out of my body, like you'd pull a silk handkerchief out of a pocket by one corner. . . . It flew around and then came back and went in again. . . ." Hemingway used this experience in *A Farewell to Arms*, a novel based on his war experiences.

connected with his body. As his physical condition grew worse, "the B consciousness began to disintegrate, while the A consciousness which was now me, seemed to be altogether *outside of my body, which I could see.*"

At this stage the physician, like the Reverend Bertrand, became clairvoyant in his second body. "Gradually I realized that I could see not only my body and the bed in which it was, but everything in the whole house and garden," he said, "and then I realized that I was seeing not only things at home, but in London and in Scotland, in fact wherever my attention was directed. . . . And the explanation which I received (from what source I do not know, but which I found myself calling to myself *my mentor*) was that I was free in a time dimension of space, wherein *now* was equivalent to *here* in the ordinary three-dimensional space of everyday life." His mentor further explained that there was a "psychic stream" flowing through the three-, four- and five-dimensional Universes, and that individual brains were "just end-organs projecting as it were from the three-dimensional Universe into the psychic stream." The different dimensions interpenetrated each other, and "the fourth dimension was in everything existing in the three-dimensional space, and at the same time everything in the three-dimensional space existed in the fourth dimension, and also in the fifth dimension.

With his clairvoyant vision, the physician began to recognize people in the three-dimensional world, and he noticed that they all had around them "psychic condensation" or auras of different colors and of varying bulk, sharpness of outline, and apparent solidity. Then he saw a friend enter his bedroom, register shock, and hurry to the telephone. He also saw his doctor receive the news, hurriedly leave his patients, and rush to his bedside and examine him. He heard his doctor say, "He is nearly gone," and watched him take a syringe and inject his body with something that he later learned was camphor. Like the Reverend Bertrand he didn't want to return to the physical. "As my heart began to beat more strongly, I was drawn back, and I was intensely annoyed because I was so interested and was just beginning to understand where I was and what I was seeing. I came back into my body, really angry at being pulled back, and once back, all the clarity of vision of anything and everything disappeared, and I was just possessed of a glimmer of consciousness which was suffused with pain."

Geddes invited his colleagues to consider the implications of this experience, and assured them: "Of one thing only can we be quite sure—it was not fake." He said that it had helped him "to define the idea of a psychic continuum, spread out in time like a plasmic net." Furthermore, he believed that it brought "telepathy, clairvoyance, Spiritualism, and indeed all the parapsychic manifestations into the domain of the picturable." These were bold words for an eminent professor to utter in the presence of professional colleagues in 1937. That Geddes ventured so to commit himself and to face possible derision surely indicates that the experience and the understanding he gained through it made a profound impression on him.

Our final false death case was reported as "The Case of Dr. X" in the *Journal of the Society for Psychical Research* in 1957. Dr. X was able to describe in detail what other people were doing at a time when his physical body was so located that he would not have been able to obtain the information by means of his normal sensory faculties, even if he had been in possession of them. He wrote his account 40 years after the event had occurred in 1916, and his memory remained clear as to exactly what had happened.

Dr. X, a medical officer with the Royal Flying Corps, crashed seconds after taking off in a small plane from a country airport. He was hurled to the ground where he lay inert and apparently dead. He experienced the abrupt separation of his second body, which seemed to rise to a height of about 200 feet above the scene of the crash. He saw the ambulance leave the airport and a crowd of anxious people gather around him. He next had a sensation of traveling at great speed through the air until he was over the Atlantic. Suddenly he was pulled back into his physical body and regained consciousness. Later, every detail of his account of what had happened after the crash while he was unconscious was confirmed by the other people concerned.

The cases of the Reverend Bertrand, Ritchie, Dr. X and Geddes—whether about himself or someone else as he said—constitute a small sample out of hundreds of recorded false deaths which have been investigated by psychical researchers. Even in this small sample, however, a number of common characteristics stand out, which are typical of many of the accounts of astral projection. All four narrators describe the same sensation of seeing their physical body from a distance, though only one, the Reverend Bertrand, mentions the exist-

Flying Doctor

Dr. X was a medical officer in World War I, and was stationed on a small country airfield in England. One day word came through that a pilot had been shot down at another airfield. Could Dr. X help to release him from the wreckage?

It was to be an event unique in the history of aviation—the first time that medical help had been taken by air to a casualty. All the top personnel turned up at the runway.

Seconds after takeoff, the plane crashed. Dr. X was thrown out into a dip where the airfield was obscured from view. Suddenly he found himself hovering about 200 feet above his unconscious body in a state of pleasant awareness. He could see the frenzied activity at the airfield. The ambulance stalled. The medical orderly jumped in. Others were running to the crash.

Then Dr. X began to move in what seemed like a delightful journey over the countryside and sea till he felt a kind of retraction and was back again hovering over his body. Then, with a pop, he was aware of an orderly pouring sal volatile down his throat. Later, all the incidents he had seen at the airfield while in his astral body were confirmed by others. Dr. X found the experience so pleasant that it completely removed his fear of death.

ence of an attenuating cord or cable between the physical and astral bodies. Both Ritchie and Dr. X reported the feeling of rapid travel, and Ritchie and the physician recorded by Geddes described the feeling that it was only necessary to will oneself to a place to be there. Ritchie and Geddes' physician also believed that they had become aware of other worlds, and had gained in knowledge through their astral experience.

From the similarities between these experiences and those of many other astral projectors it would seem reasonable to class the OOBE as a genuine psychic phenomenon. In these examples it has been associated with the process of dying, but there is another class of evidence: that of people who have experienced separation while under the influence of anesthetics or drugs. In their book, *The Phenomena of Astral Projection*, Muldoon and Carrington wrote: "Anesthetics, producing deep unconsciousness, are . . . ideal for producing astral projection." They also said that although anesthesia was a state of total blankness for most people, "there are many cases on record in which, seemingly, more or less complete consciousness has been retained by the patient, and he has afterwards been enabled to describe all that went on in the operating room, the conversation of the physicians and nurses, and any unusual details which may have developed."

A British surgeon, George Sava, published a volume of reminiscences and reflections in 1953 entitled *A Surgeon Remembers*. In it he says, "It is indeed a disquieting thought . . . that every time one operates, one's activities are under observation from the patient's astral body hovering overhead . . . a fascinating but frightening possibility." The experience that gave rise to these thoughts was connected with an operation he had once performed on an elderly woman, Mrs. Frances Gail.

Mrs. Gail was in a postoperative coma and seemed to be sinking fast. An urgent call from the hospital brought Dr. Sava from his home, and he worked hard to bring his patient back to consciousness. He was successful, and when she was able to speak Mrs. Gail told him that she had been out of her body and would have preferred to have remained out of it, but she had come back because her friends had called her. Sava was sympathetic but, of course, not particularly impressed by this information, which could be merely an old person's subjective fantasy, but what she said next astounded him.

"You didn't carry out the operation you first intended, did you, Mr. Sava? . . . You kept my body lying there under the anesthetic while you and the others discussed whether it was strong enough to withstand what you proposed to do. You took away some pieces of bone. You were chiefly troubled about the anesthetic and said to the anesthetist: 'Do you think she can stand three hours of it? Heart all right?' The anesthetist just nodded and said, 'She's okay, especially considering she's no chicken.' Is that right?"

It was right. Every detail of Frances Gail's account exactly corresponded with what had happened in the operating theater while she had been under the anesthetic. It was told as an attentive and fully conscious observer might have told it.

A similar experience is recalled by Dr. Russell MacRobert, a

Right: this drawing by Sylvia Leone Mahler (real name Edith Haubold) is entitled *Alpha* and shows man linked to a higher plane of existence via a looped and spiraling cord. While hospitalized after a major operation Sylvia Mahler had her first out-of-the-body experience. She was in pain and about to ring for a painkiller when she began to feel as though the room had faded away. She seemed to be standing at the bottom of a deep well, constructed of transparent leaves, rocks, shells, and flowers, all in beautiful colors. She began to rise upward through the well, observing fascinating and beautiful shapes and colors, until she reached the interior of a vast cathedral, decorated on the walls with intricate designs. Faced by unknown beings who gazed at her, she felt an immediate urge "to declare . . . my dedication forevermore to that indescribable glory for which there is no single name." At that moment, the nurse awakened her to give her an injection. But for those moments she had been "in a world beyond the boundaries of pain . . . containing the greatest joy I have ever experienced." After this occasion she turned to art, finding it a way to express her new insights.

staff doctor at the Lennox Hill Hospital in New York City. The patient in this case was a clergyman who was having an ear operation. He was in great pain and was given extra anesthetic for the operation. The surgeon was just about to begin when he discovered that he was lacking a necessary special instrument. He swore, took off his gloves, and went to get his instrument bag from another room down the hall. When he returned he put on fresh gloves and a gown, had a nurse sterilize the instrument, and started the operation.

All this time, and throughout the operation, the surgeon and his assistants were apparently being observed by the patient, who was fascinated by the proceedings. When he came round from the anesthetic he was able to give a detailed account of what had happened. He could repeat everything that had been said and tell the nurses exactly the positions they had occupied at all times during the operation. He informed the surgeon that he had accompanied him on his trip down the hall, and good-humoredly chided him for swearing in front of a clergyman.

Among Dr. Crookall's voluminous records of astral projection, there are many cases of OOBEs under anesthetic. Generally subjects are too interested in watching what is being done to

Above: this wooden sculpture depicts Belam, a spirit of the Melanau tribe of Sarawak, in Malaysia. Belam is believed to catch the souls of sick people and restore them to their bodies. This is a variation on the widespread belief among primitive peoples that illness is caused by a separation of the astral and physical bodies.

Below: an Australian aboriginal bark painting depicting a funeral ceremony and the path of the wandering spirit after death. The path is a symbol common to many cultures, both primitive and civilized.

their physical body to leave the scene of the operation; but in one of Crookall's cases the patient took a casual glance at her body, and left the surgeon to go on with his job as she went off to see what members of her family were doing. She saw her husband waiting in a corridor in the hospital for news of her. She wondered what her daughter was doing, and the thought projected her into a shop where her daughter was choosing a get well card for her. Over the unsuspecting girl's shoulder she read the texts of two cards the daughter was choosing between. She watched her reject the card with the more flippant text and buy the other. Then she returned to her physical body in the hospital. When the operation was over and she was able to receive visitors, her daughter came in carrying the get well card in an envelope. She was astonished when her mother recited the text before opening the card, and even more astonished to be told the words on the card she had rejected.

It may be said that these cases could all be accounted for by extrasensory perception functioning in some way in the unconscious, and that they are not evidence for the projection or survival of the etheric body. But in some cases the body has been seen by others. A Chicago physician, Dr. Hout, who had himself

Below: a picture entitled *Two Paths* by Huichol shaman Ramon Medina. These vivid pictures, which have been made by this Mexican tribe for generations, depict many of their magical beliefs, as well as visions induced by the drug peyote. This example shows the two paths taken by departed spirits: the one at right is for transgressors against sexual taboos and is lined with purifying fire, two rocks between which it must slip, and a hot, foul-smelling pool. The one at left, for the virtuous, has more ambiguous symbols—a crow that refuses to eat the hungry soul and a pool of clear water.

Above: *The Departure of the Astral Body at Death*, an engraving based on a clairvoyant vision of the 19th-century American mystic Andrew Jackson Davis. There are many accounts of people seeing a spirit—or something—leave the body of a dying person. Left: an Etruscan wall-painting showing the Furies carrying away the soul of a dead person. Here the soul is depicted as a fairly solid-looking figure but without arms. Originally conceived by the Greeks as malevolent and bloodthirsty beings, the Furies eventually assumed a milder identity.

experienced projections, wrote in the American monthly magazine *Prediction* that one day he "was privileged to see the spirit counterparts" of three patients who had operations under anesthetic. Soon after the first patient, an elderly woman, was brought into the surgery, he saw a form rise and float free in space above the operating table. And "as the anesthetic deepened and the physical body became more relaxed, the freedom of the spirit body became greater. For the spirit form floated more freely away from the physical counterpart during the height of the anesthetic. . . . The spirit was quiet, as though it was also in deep peaceful sleep. I knew that the direct process of surgical activity was not affecting it. . . . At the finish of this operation, while the wound was being closed, the spirit came closer to the body but had not yet reentered its vehicle when the patient was wheeled from the operating theater." In this and in the other two cases, Dr. Hout wrote, he saw the cord connecting the physical and etheric bodies, and it looked like "a silvery shaft of light which wound around through the room in much the same way as a curl of smoke will drift indifferently in still atmosphere."

Left: *The Soul of St. Bertin Carried up to God*, a 15th-century painting showing the ascent of a holy man's soul as conceived by medieval Christianity. The artists of the late Middle Ages delighted in painting rich textures, and their portrayals of the afterlife are just as solid and sensuous as their portrayals of the concrete, physical world.

Crookall has collected many accounts of people seeing the second body leaving the physical body at death. Common features of these accounts are that the vaporous substance emerges from the head, gradually condenses into a form resembling the physical body, remains connected for a time with the physical by means of the silvery cord, and then disappears. A British nurse and psychic, Joy Snell, wrote in 1918 in her book *The Ministry of Angels* that she had often observed this phenomenon. She described the death of a close friend in this way: "Immediately after her heart had ceased to beat, I distinctly saw something in appearance like smoke . . . ascend from her body. . . . This form, shadowy at first, gradually changed and . . . resolved itself into a form like that of my friend but glorified, with no trace on it of the spasm of pain which had seized her just before she died."

Muldoon and Carrington quote the testimony of a missionary who spent many years in Tahiti. He reported that the Tahitians believe that at death the soul is drawn out of the body via the head, and that their clairvoyants described the process of separation in exactly the same terms as their European and American counterparts have described it. Such cross-cultural similarity strongly suggests that the phenomenon is not merely hallucinatory.

In his monograph *Deathbed Observations by Physicians and Nurses*, Dr. K. Osis of the American Society for Psychical Research has assembled a great deal of evidence that supports the view that death is an altered state of consciousness, and that for many people it is attended by experiences of exaltation and ecstasy. The testimonies of people who have experienced false deaths confirm this. The accounts given by Geddes and Ritchie as to the existence of other worlds or dimensions of reality cannot just be lightly shrugged off. Both Osis and Crookall have records of deathbed visions in which the dying person has met and sometimes been "helped over" by a friend or relative who neither he nor anybody present knew at the time was dead. The evidence for some kind of existence "beyond the veil" is strong, and the day will come for each of us when we have the opportunity to conduct our own personal investigation.

Left: Dr. Karlis Osis, director of research at the American Society for Psychical Research. The apparatus behind him is his own invention, a "soul trap," which is intended to detect out-of-the-body projection. The subject sits in another room, wired to an EEG, and attempts to view, in the astral body, the image inside the hole.

Right: three photographs purporting to show the soul leaving the body at death. They were taken early in this century by the French physician Hippolyte Baraduc and show his wife (top), 15 minutes after death, and (middle) one hour after death, and (bottom) his son's body photographed in the coffin nine hours after death.

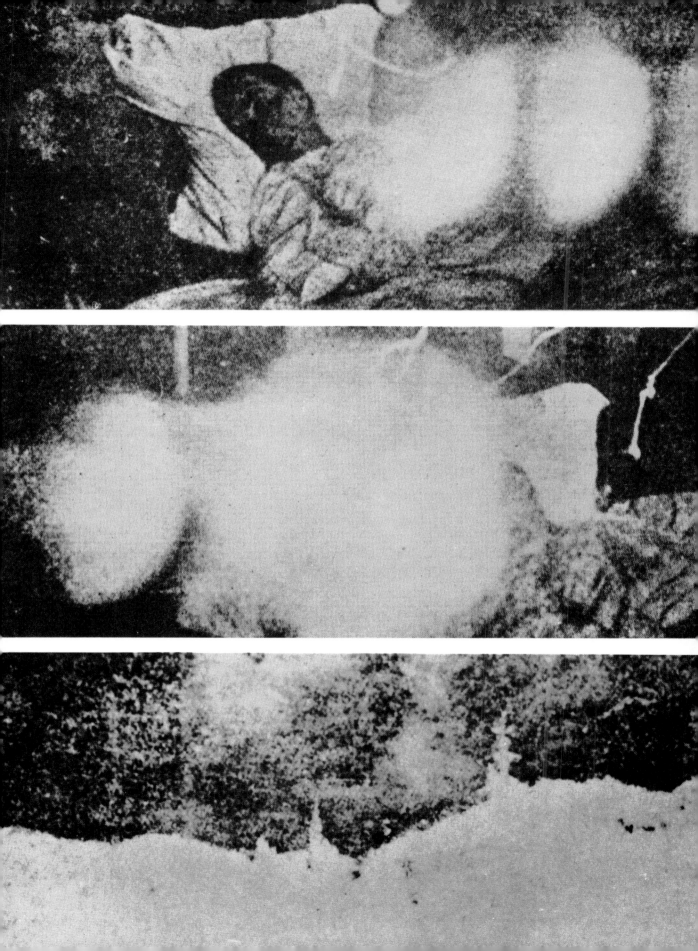

6

Possession and Multiple Personality

In 1944 the widow of a famous Brazilian author, Humberto de Campos, sued in court for a share in the royalties of five books that her husband had written after his death. The books had issued from the pen of Chico Xavier, a prolific trance-writer, who did not contest the fact that they were the dead man's creation. He even offered to go into trance and produce more specimens of de Campos' work right in the courtroom. Distinguished critics vouched for the fact that the books were typical of the alleged author in style and subject matter. The judge, however, ruled that the dead had no rights in courts of law, and dismissed the widow's suit. The case of

Right: this was painted by a British housewife named Madge Gill who, before her death in 1961, produced hundreds of drawings and paintings while she was in a state of semitrance. Mrs. Gill believed herself "undoubtedly guided by an unseen force" and attributed many of her works to a spirit she called Myrninerest.

"The dead sometimes take possession of the living and use them"

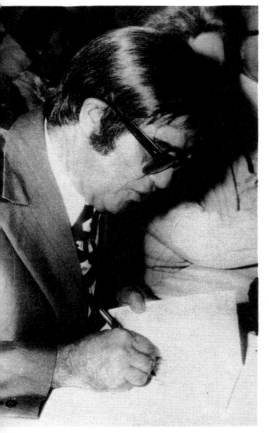

Below: the Brazilian medium and automatic writer "Chico" Xavier, born in 1910. By the age of 64, he had written 126 books that he claims are actually written by a number of "spiritual entities." His works include novels, essays, history, and works on the teachings of Spiritism (Spiritualism).

Chico Xavier is one of many which suggest that the dead sometimes take possession of the living, and use them as instruments for communication or action in the present world. Although psychological explanations of the phenomena of possession, multiple personality, and the command of unknown languages can often be advanced, there are many cases that do not easily yield to such explanations. That of Chico Xavier is one of them.

Before he died, de Campos himself vouched for the apparent authenticity of one of Xavier's published works, a 421-page volume purporting to be a collection of poems by Brazil's greatest dead poets. De Campos wrote that the alleged authors of these poems showed in them "the same characteristics of inspiration and expression that identified them on this planet." He also said: "The themes they tackle are those that preoccupied them when alive. The taste is the same, and the verse generally obeys the same musical flow." For Xavier to have produced the work out of his own head would have been a prodigious feat of literary parody, and one for which he was hardly educationally equipped. He had left school at 13 and had worked in a textile factory, as a kitchen hand, and as a salesman before settling in a modest clerical post in the civil service, which he retained until he retired in 1961.

Xavier is still busy trance writing today, and up to 1974 he had produced 126 books in many categories including poetry, fiction, children's books, history, popular science, and doctrine of Spiritualism, or Spiritism as it is known in Brazil. Immense industry and erudition, apart from literary genius, would have been required for any one man to have created this great variety of work. Xavier has suffered from defective eyesight all his life, and can read only slowly and with difficulty. He could hardly have acquired by normal means the vast knowledge that has gone into his books. He has stated that he scarcely understands a word of some of the scientific writings that have flowed from his pen. Since he doesn't claim authorship of any of the work, he has donated the substantial income from the books to the Spiritist cause.

In 1958 Xavier and another Brazilian Spiritist trance-author jointly produced over a period of 40 days a book entitled *Evolution in Two Worlds*. The discarnate, or nonphysical, author of this work seems to have wanted to prove his authorship because he divided the chapters of his book between Xavier and the second writer, Dr. Waldo Vieira, alternating between them. The two trance-writers lived 250 miles apart and were not in communication during the book's composition. Guy Playfair, who has a chapter on Xavier in his book *The Flying Cow*, says that *Evolution in Two Worlds* "reveals an immense knowledge of several sciences that no ordinary writer, even a qualified scientist, could have assembled without copious research and note-taking, and despite the wide education gap between the two writers, the unity of style is total. One chapter frequently begins where the previous one leaves off."

The phenomena of automatic writing and trance mediumship are generally fairly benevolent forms of spirit possession. Both are to some extent controlled by the mediums, at least in so far as they deliberately go into trance and temporarily allow themselves to be taken over for use as an instrument or channel. But the term "possession" is normally used to stand for something more sinister: a total and uncontrollable usurpation of a personality by an invading entity. Of course, to speak of an invading entity is to put a Spiritualist interpretation on the facts, whereas many psychologists would maintain that possession is really acute schizophrenia, and that the forces that usurp the victim's personality originate within his or her own unconscious. There are some cases of alleged possession, however, which contain elements that are difficult to explain in terms of abnormal psychology.

In May 1922 an American minister and psychologist, Walter Franklin Prince, was approached by a certain Mrs. Latimer, a woman he later described as "highly cultivated." She was convinced that for two years she had been possessed and tormented by the spirit of a cousin by the name of Marvin. It had begun a few days after Marvin's death when she had distinctly heard his voice saying, "You made me suffer and I will make you suffer." This sentence was to be repeated often over subsequent months. She didn't understand how she had made Marvin suffer until he reminded her of a letter she had written shortly before his death in which she had made a disparaging remark about him. It was true, although she was certain that Marvin couldn't have seen the letter. She was also accused by the spirit of having failed to send flowers for his coffin. She had in fact sent roses, but when she checked she found that they had been placed inconspicuously away from the coffin itself.

Below: Dr. Walter Franklin Prince (right), the American psychical researcher, talking with a farmer, Alexander McDonald, whose family were driven from their farmhouse by ghosts. Dr. Prince once succeeded in freeing a woman from what seemed to be a spirit that possessed and tormented her.

Over the two years before she consulted Prince, Mrs. Latimer had hardly had a single night when she didn't wake up screaming loudly and uncontrollably. Her days were also tormented. Marvin often correctly predicted how she would be hurt by the attitudes or actions of other people. He threatened that the torments would continue until she made a sincere mental apology, which she felt unable to do.

Prince had some experience of treating people with troubles of a psychic nature, in the course of which he had found that conventional psychiatric methods of depth analysis combined with persuasion and suggestion were of no avail. He decided to try the experiment of acting on the assumption that Mrs. Latimer really was possessed by the spirit of Marvin, and of giving treatment by lecturing the vindictive spirit.

"I wish to talk with you as one gentleman talks to another," Prince began solemnly, and in Mrs. Latimer's presence he proceeded to give Marvin a 15-minute lecture. He reasoned with him and exhorted him to change his ways. "I shall not deny that you may have had provocation," he said, ". . . but feel sure that you are . . . preventing your own development and progress . . . Your habit of ill will against this woman results in what is called her possession. In fact, you yourself are obsessed by the habit . . ." He suggested that Marvin had probably brooded over his cousin's offense during his last hours, giving it an importance far greater than it deserved, and that he should now review the whole matter intelligently and forgive her. If he did so, Prince said, "the time will come when your life will become so transformed that you will be very thankful for the suggestion I make today."

Prince's unconventional strategy worked quickly. Mrs. Latimer's torments ceased. Her first night's sleep after the session with Prince was disturbed only by a dream in which her dead mother appeared and said, "We heard what the man said. I will take care of Marvin. Go to sleep." On two successive nights Marvin appeared to her in her sleep and, she said, "just stood silently and sorrowfully." When she returned for another consultation with Prince and told him what had happened, he addressed the spirit again and solemnly congratulated him. Mrs. Latimer only heard the voice on one or two more occasions, and on one of these Marvin explained that he had been unable to free himself of the embittered thoughts toward her that had preoccupied him at the time of his death, and that in tormenting her he had been urged on by other vindictive spirits. He promised that he would soon be gone. Mrs. Latimer suffered from vague feelings of unease and tiredness for some months. One day something told her, "You are now free," and thereafter she showed no further symptoms of possession or psychic illness.

Did Prince cure his patient by playing along with her delusion and giving her suggestions that enabled her to free herself of it? Or did he really exorcise a possessing spirit? He did not profess to know the answer himself, though he was impressed by the fact that so quick and complete a cure was effected without anything being done or said directly to the patient. Some time later he repeated the experiment with Leonard Tyrrell, who was being tormented by a deceased acquaintance named Murray. Again

Prince gave his no-nonsense, man-to-man speech, to which Murray responded through Tyrrell's automatic writing: "Well, there may be something in what you say; I had never thought of it in that light before. I'll think about it. You may tell him I won't trouble him this week." In a later consultation Murray wrote that he was grateful to Prince for his suggestions because he was now making progress on his side, and he wouldn't disturb Tyrrell again. Sure enough, the symptoms instantly ceased. If it was psychotherapy, it was unlike any other psychotherapy in its simplicity and instant effectiveness.

It is difficult to find any psychological theories that would explain the facts of the classic case of possession, the "Watseka Wonder" case. It is an old case, but it was investigated and authenticated at the time by Richard Hodgson, a psychical researcher who was as thorough, knowledgeable, and skeptical about the supernatural as any modern psychologist.

Mary Roff had died at the age of 18, 12 years before the events occurred that seemed to give evidence of her reappearance in her home town of Watseka, Illinois. The bereaved Roffs were neighbors of the Vennums, and for four months in 1878 14-year-old Lurancy Vennums was apparently possessed by the spirit of Mary, who had died when Lurancy was 15 months old. When the possession started Lurancy was so unhappy with her own family that her parents sent her to the Roffs. She greeted everyone with delight using the familiar names, and sometimes nicknames, by which Mary had known them in her childhood. When she was asked how long she would stay, she answered, "The angels will let me stay till some time in May."

During those months hundreds of little incidents occurred which convinced the Roffs beyond doubt that their daughter had returned in the borrowed body of Lurancy Vennums. The child had total recall of virtually everything that had happened to Mary in her lifetime years before. She remembered minor accidents, journeys, family events and habits in minute detail. On one occasion while the child was out, Mr. Roff asked his wife to find a certain velvet headdress that Mary had habitually worn in the last year of her life, and put it on a stand. Mrs. Roff did so, and when the girl returned she immediately noticed it and said, "Oh, there is my headdress I wore when my hair was short." Then she asked if her mother had kept a certain box with letters in it, and when Mrs. Roff produced the box the girl found among its contents a piece of material and said delightedly, "Oh, ma, here is a collar I tatted! Ma, why did you not show to me my letters and things before?"

On May 21 Mary said fond farewells to her family and Lurancy Vennums returned to her own family. Her own personality and memories were restored, and she settled down happily in her former surroundings.

Richard Hodgson, who visited the Roffs' home several times while Lurancy was there, wrote that there were two possible explanations. Either Lurancy had a secondary personality endowed with supernormal powers of telepathy, clairvoyance, and retrocognition, or she really was possessed for those four months by the spirit of Mary Roff. Hodgson, one of the least credulous of men involved in psychical research, admitted that he had

Above: the American psychical investigator Richard Hodgson, who studied the case of Lurancy Vennums, a teenage girl who was apparently possessed by the spirit of a neighbor who had died at the age of 18, when Lurancy herself was only 15 months old. Hodgson finally came to the conclusion that the case belonged "to the spiritist category" and was not a case of multiple personality.

Above: a self-portrait by Hélène Smith showing her with her guardian angel. She claimed to have experienced astral travel and to have visited Mars. Flournoy attributed her experiences to the workings of her subconscious mind.

formed the personal opinion that the case belonged "to the spiritistic category."

Over the past 80 years some 150 cases of multiple personality have been reported, and invariably they have given rise to debate between the psychologists and the Spiritualists. The psychologists' case was perhaps best put by Theodor Flournoy. Born in 1854, he became Professor of Psychology at the University of Geneva. In a book entitled *Spiritualism and Psychology* he wrote: "As a crystal splits under the blow of a hammer when struck according to certain definite lines of cleavage, in the same way the human personality, under the shock of excessive emotions, is sometimes broken along the lines of least resistance or the great structural lines of his temperament. A cleavage is produced between opposite selves—whose harmonious equilibrium would constitute the normal condition—seriousness and gaiety; optimistic tendencies and pessimistic; goodness and egoism; instinct of prudery and lasciviousness; the taste for solitude and the love of Nature, and the attraction of civilization etc. The differences, in which the Spiritists see a striking proof of an absolute distinction between the spirits and their so-called instruments, awaken, on the contrary, in the mind of the psychologist the irresistible suspicion that these pretended spirits can be nothing but the products of the subconsciousness of the medium himself."

This is plausible, but it is an argument that rests on faith just as much as the Spiritualist case does. One man who was not satisfied with the psychological explanations of the phenomenon of multiple personality was James Hyslop, Professor of Logic and Ethics at Columbia University in New York City. Also born in 1854, he became an active psychical researcher. He devised a method of separating material of subconscious origin from material of external origin in multiple personality. He would take the subject to a medium who had no prior knowledge of the case. If the medium channeled information or manifested characteristics corresponding to those of the alien personality that was intermittently taking possession of the subject, Hyslop considered that there was a strong probability that the other personality really was alien and of external origin. He tried this experiment with several patients and eventually reached the conclusion—which he said he "fought against for 10 years"—that in certain cases traditionally ascribed to hysteria, multiple personality,

Âme

Je veux tenir ma promesse mais tu comprendras sans nul te, qu'aujourd'hui à cet instant je suis forcé d'être d'une grande et dois m'abstenir de beaucoup

Below: an automatic drawing made around 1870 by Mrs. Alaric Watts, a medium. She tried at first to repress her automatic drawing, as she had done with automatic writing: later, she decided that the visions that inspired her work conveyed religious truths. Unlike many automatic artists, Mrs. Watts was a capable artist while normally conscious. This visionary drawing uses watercolors and colored inks applied with a reed pen to tracing paper.

paranoia, or some other form of mental disturbance, there were strong indications that the person had, in fact, been invaded by foreign or nonphysical agencies.

One of the most famous cases of multiple personality was that of Miss Beauchamp, investigated by the psychologist Dr. Morton Prince. After a series of emotional shocks, Miss Beauchamp developed four distinct personalities each of which differed in health, in knowledge, and in memories. The third personality, Sally, claimed to be a spirit, and she dominated and could hypnotize the others, sometimes tormenting them mischievously. She put toads and spiders into a box so that the first self would get a shock when she opened it. She took the last public transportation of the day to its terminus in the country and left the first self to walk back to town. She took a particular dislike to the fourth personality and maliciously persecuted her. When Prince tried to integrate the four personalities into one with hypnotic suggestion, Sally remained resistant and independent, always insisting that she was a spirit. Prince then tried the technique that Walter Franklin Prince had used in the Latimer and Tyrrell cases. He reasoned and exhorted. Finally Sally agreed to be squeezed out of existence, and the remaining three personalities were successfully welded into one.

Walter Franklin Prince treated a similar case, that of Doris Fischer, in which one of the personalities was mischievously dominant and seemed more like an invading entity than a projection from the unconscious. In this case there were five personalities involved. They were called Real Doris, Margaret, Sleeping Margaret, Sick Doris, and Sleeping Doris. Margaret was the independent spirit. She stole so that Real Doris would be blamed, hid her school books, jumped into a filthy river with her clothes on, and scratched her body until it bled, leaving Real Doris to suffer the pain. The torments went on for years. James Hyslop cooperated with Prince to treat Doris Fischer, and it was one of the cases in which the assistance of a medium was sought. Corroborative evidence came through suggesting invasion by foreign or nonphysical agencies.

Two modern cases of multiple personality that became well known outside medical literature are the cases of Eve and of Bridey Murphy. The case history of Eve was described in *The Three Faces of Eve*, a book by the two psychiatrists C. H. Tigpen and H. M. Cleckley. Later it became a successful film. Eve White, a married woman with one child, was sent for psychiatric treatment because of persistent headaches and occasional blackouts. She was described as "a neat colorless woman." Orthodox treatment relieved her symptoms, but not long after it was discontinued Eve returned to her psychiatrists. She was sent by her enraged husband because she had been on an expensive shopping spree and had bought a wardrobe of sexy clothes, though she had no recollection of the event. During an interview with the doctors, Eve suddenly changed personality. A "bright unfamiliar voice that sparkled" said "Hi, there, doc!" and Eve Black appeared. Eve Black was contemptuous of Eve White and knew everything about her. She said she had often used her blackouts in order to get out and enjoy herself, go to bars, flirt with men, and buy expensive clothes. Eve White knew nothing of this other self.

Above: James Hyslop, Professor of Logic and Ethics at Columbia University in the late 1800s. His studies of mediums and of people said to be suffering from hysteria or multiple personality led him finally to believe that there was such a thing as possession of a person by an alien spirit.

Left: one of a series of drawings and paintings by Ethel le Rossignol that she claims were created by the spirit of a friend who died and who told her, through automatic writing and through the drawings, what the afterlife is like. This drawing, entitled *The Lover of All Men Is Now Freed from the Body*, shows the soul of one who has achieved wisdom now linked with other souls by the "Girdle of Glory," which is the "current of Love and Wisdom." He is "led to the gates of Heaven, where the light of the aura is woven into a harmony of azure, green, gold and mauve."

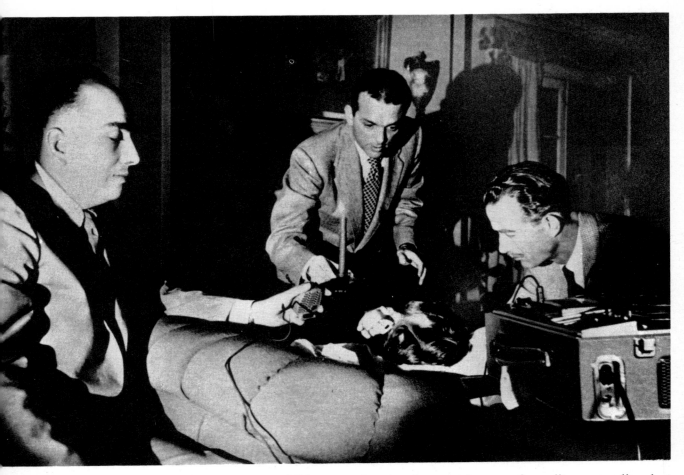

Above: Morey Bernstein, an amateur hypnotist and writer, hypnotizing Virginia Tighe, a Colorado housewife who—while in hypnotic trance—apparently relived an earlier life as an Irishwoman named Bridey Murphy. Bernstein's book *The Search for Bridey Murphy* contained a wealth of details of life in Ireland recalled by Mrs. Tighe (called Ruth Simmons in the book); but later investigation suggested that childhood memories may have produced the material.

This seemed a simple enough case of a split personality, but during the next stage of therapy a third personality emerged. This one, who called herself Jane, professed to know nothing at all about Eve White or Eve Black. Jane was a more aware, intelligent, and integrated personality than either of the two Eves. Although they never became aware of her existence she got to know them both well. She accompanied them wherever they went, observed them closely, and showed sympathy with them over their problems. This weird situation in which Eve White knew nothing about her other two personalities, Eve Black knew all about Eve White but didn't suspect the existence of Jane, and Jane knew about both of the others, continued for about a year. Then the three became integrated around the predominant personality of Jane, which was a happy outcome for all concerned.

The case of Eve does not challenge the psychologists' contention that the phenomenon of multiple personality is a psychological and not a spiritual one, because the two new personalities that emerged during therapy could plausibly have been respectively repressed and undeveloped aspects of Eve's own personality. In fact, the thought might occur to some people that the case is as well known as it is precisely because it so neatly illustrates the psychologists' case.

In 1956 a book entitled *The Search for Bridey Murphy* became a best-seller. It was written by an amateur hypnotist, Morey Bernstein, of Pueblo, Colorado. Bernstein had read about other

Left: Virginia Tighe as a young woman in the 1950s. As "Bridey Murphy," she had supposedly lived in Ireland between 1798 and 1864. One thing that made her case convincing—apart from the many accurate details it included—was the prosaic nature of Bridey's life. Many—if not most—people who claim to be reincarnated insist that in their previous lives they were royalty or great artists, giving their accounts an element of wishful thinking.

Right: Virginia Tighe at the age of seven. During her first hypnotic sessions with Bernstein she regressed to the age of one year.

Below: the actress Teresa Wright portraying Virginia Tighe under hypnosis in the film based on the story of Bridey Murphy. While hypnotized, "Bridey" remembered not only details of her life but also her own funeral in Belfast. Investigation in Ireland confirmed the accuracy of many of the terms and figures of speech she used, but failed to discover any conclusive evidence of her existence.

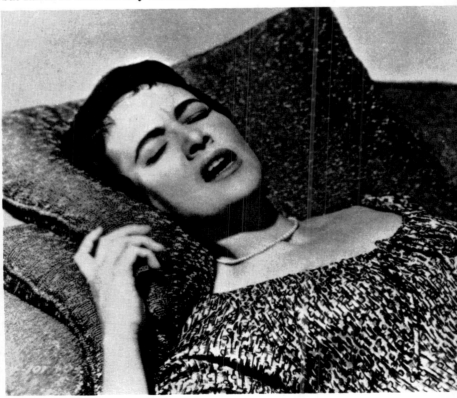

hypnotists employing age-regression techniques to get information about previous incarnations, and one evening in 1952 he tried the experiment on a friend, Virginia Tighe. Under deep hypnosis, she suddenly became a completely different personality. She spoke with a distinct Irish brogue and claimed to be Bridey Murphy, who had lived in Cork, Ireland between 1798 and 1864. Over six separate sessions, Bernstein elicited a great deal of information from Bridey, including descriptions of Irish scenes and customs and a number of colloquial expressions. Virginia had never been to Ireland, and it seemed extremely unlikely that she could have obtained the information in any normal way. However, when psychologists studied the material after the publication of Bernstein's book, they discovered that there were experiences in Virginia Tighe's past that resembled material in Bridey's communications. For instance, her childhood home was found to have had many features in common with the house in Cork as described by Bridey. The discovery of such similarities quickly led to the case being discredited, and Bernstein paid the price often exacted of those who enjoy overnight fame. However, Professor C. J. Ducasse of Brown University in Rhode Island, who studied the material carefully, defended Bernstein and Virginia Tighe, and publicly declared his conviction that there was no fraud involved in the Bridey Murphy case.

The emergence of other personalities, allegedly from past lives, when a person is under deep hypnosis is not a phenomenon confined to the Bridey Murphy case. An English hypnotist, Arnall Bloxham, has conducted age-regression experiments with

Below: English hypnotist Arnall Bloxham, putting a subject into a trance. He has taken many people back in time to relive previous lives. He and his wife are convinced that all of us pass through several reincarnations until—as in Hindu and Buddhist teaching— we attain a state of perfection.

several subjects. His book, *Who Was Ann Ockenden?*, published in 1958 contains impressive circumstantial detail, obtained from a young girl under hypnosis, of a previous existence in prehistoric times. Another of his subjects regressed to the 17th century and claimed to be Henriette, sister of Charles II of England and wife of Philippe, Duke of Orleans. She was able to describe details of daily life at the court of Louis XIV of France. A third subject, a man, remembered his previous life as a naval gunner during the Napoleonic wars, and experts on naval history who have listened to Bloxham's tapes of his sessions with this subject have been profoundly impressed by their authenticity of detail.

Several other hypnotists have come up with material similar to Bernstein's and Bloxham's, which on the face of it looks like evidence for reincarnation. Some psychologists have not taken the easy way of glibly dismissing the phenomenon as fraud, but have been disinclined to accept the reincarnation explanation of it. These have suggested two alternative hypotheses: the workings of unconscious memory or of extrasensory perception. According to the unconscious memory theory, people may, at some time in the past, have registered information that comes through under hypnosis without being aware of it. They may, for instance, have flicked through a book and subliminally photographed and stored away pages of its contents. The ESP hypothesis holds that the information may have been culled from the minds of others telepathically and without awareness that it was happening. Up to the present, no systematic research has been devised in age-regression experiments that excludes these possibilities.

History Relived

Arthur Guirdham is an English psychiatrist. For over 40 years he was afflicted by a recurring nightmare in which a tall man approached him.

Then one day in 1962 a woman patient came to see him and described a nightmare similar to his own. Dr. Guirdham did not tell her of his own dream; but oddly, it never recurred after that. As the woman, whom he calls Mrs. Smith, continued treatment she revealed strange facts about her life: her ability to predict the future and her detailed dreams of life in the southern part of France during the Middle Ages as a member of an heretical sect called the Cathars. She did not at first tell the doctor that she immediately recognized him as her lover, Roger de Grisolles, in those dreams.

It is not unusual for a psychiatric patient to have sexual fantasies about the doctor. But Mrs. Smith's recollections of medieval France, of the persecutions suffered by her coreligionists, and of being herself burned at the stake were extraordinarily detailed. Guirdham had details from them checked by medieval historians, and the most obscure of them were corroborated. Her memories struck a chord in the doctor's own psyche, and he is now convinced that he too lived as a Cathar in France.

Above: Ann Ockenden, an English schoolteacher who—according to Arnall Bloxham—has had 11 previous lives, two as women and nine as men. Her earliest memories are of life as a caveman. Critics have observed that, oddly, the foreign previous incarnations speak English, to which Mrs. Bloxham replies that "if a subject spoke in a foreign tongue the interview would end, for Arnall, not knowing what was said, could not ask the next question."

A project completed in 1971 by Alan Gauld, Professor of Psychology at the University of Nottingham in Nottingham, England, suggests a method that might be applied to checking the results of age-regression experiments, and possibly the kind of result that might be expected. Gauld worked with information supplied by "drop-in" communicators who produced information by automatic writing or at a ouija board session. Drop-in is the name given to spirit communicators who are unidentifiable, and who give information that has nothing to do with anyone present at the session. Such information is later often found to refer to real events and real people. Gauld found after very careful checking that in 10 cases out of 37, information the drop-in spirits had given about their identity and former lives was correct, even including their exact names, addresses, and previous occupations.

Unconscious memory is the explanation usually brought forward to account for the phenomenon of *xenoglossy*, or the speaking of unknown languages. It is a plausible explanation when, as in some recorded cases, a person speaks just a few phrases or verses in a foreign or ancient language, but it seems a very unlikely explanation when the language is used actively and responsively. Nobody can acquire the skill of speaking a foreign language just by mentally photographing a few pages of a book.

The classic case of xenoglossy is the Rosemary case. In 1928 a young Englishwoman suddenly started producing automatic writing. The experience rather alarmed her, so she consulted a doctor who was known to take a particular interest in psychical research. Dr. Wood reassured her, and she came to share his in-

Left: a portrait of Henriette, sister of Charles II of England and the wife of Philippe, Duke of Orleans. One of Arnall Bloxham's subjects revealed, under hypnosis, that she had been Princess Henriette in a previous existence. She disclosed many details of the court of Louis XIV, where she had lived after her marriage.

Below: a Bible-reading on board ship in the early 19th century. One of Arnall Bloxham's subjects remembered a previous life as a gunner's mate on a British ship during the Napoleonic wars. He described, under hypnosis, a battle in which he had lost a leg. At the point when he was wounded, the subject screamed as if in pain. Earl Mountbatten was so impressed by the authentic details of the sailor's account that he borrowed the tape recording and played it at a dinner to a number of experts on naval history.

terest and acted as a medium in seances with him. In one seance a communicator appeared who identified herself as Nona, an Egyptian woman who had lived about 3300 years ago. The Nona seances were held over several years, and in them Rosemary responded in a strange foreign language to questions Wood put to her in English. Nona said the language was her "mother tongue." Wood transcribed the words and phrases phonetically, and when he had obtained a substantial amount of material he showed it to an Egyptologist. That expert was not only able to translate the material, but also to confirm that it consisted of intelligible responses to Wood's questions. Part of the information communicated consisted of details of the life of Vola, a friend and contemporary of Nona's who the latter said was a previous incarnation of Rosemary's. As in Bloxham's Ann Ockenden case, it was impossible to check the circumstantial details of the alleged past incarnation. But over the years some 5000 intelligible words and phrases in ancient Egyptian came through in the communications, and were consistently pronounced in the same way: a phenomenon that defies rational psychological explanation.

In his 1966 article "Twenty Cases Suggestive of Reincarnation," Ian Stevenson, Professor of Psychiatry at the University of Virginia, writes about his own long and careful investigation of a modern case. The subject was the wife of a Philadelphia doctor who occasionally used hypnosis on his patients. One day he tried an age-regression experiment with his wife. In her first trance she had the alarming sensation of being struck on the head and drowned. Then she said, "I am a man," and gave the name "Jensen Jacoby." The communicator spoke broken English and a language that was unfamiliar to the hypnotist, but which he later learned was Swedish. In all, eight seances were held in which Jensen communicated. In the later ones Swedish-speaking people were present, and were able to ask Jensen questions in his own language. Stevenson carefully studied the tapes of the communications and discovered that although Jensen's vocabulary was very limited and he usually replied very briefly to questions, some 60 words were first introduced into the conversations by Jensen and had not been previously used by any of the interviewers. Moreover, though he lacked words for many familiar 20th-century objects, he was able to give the correct old Swedish names for museum objects from the 17th century.

Stevenson's evidence strongly suggests that the Philadelphia doctor's wife became a medium for a 17th-century Swede's communications, and more circumstantial evidence might have been obtained had not the doctor insisted on discontinuing the experiment for fear of "a permanent 'possession' or other transformation of personality." However, xenoglossy, multiple personality, and possession are at best only evidence for fragmented, partial, and temporary reincarnations. Evidence for more complete and permanent reincarnations has also been provided by Professor Stevenson, who has made it his specialty as a parapsychologist to follow up and scrupulously check and test the authenticity of reports of alleged reincarnation phenomena all over the world in our own day.

Above: an English medium called Rosemary who, while in a trance, spoke in a strange language later identified by an Egyptologist as ancient Egyptian. Translated, her speech revealed details of a life lived some 3300 years ago.

Right: a painting of the Pentecost by a 16th-century Portuguese artist. This was the event, shortly after Christ's Ascension, when the Holy Spirit descended upon the Apostles, and they began to speak in other tongues. Speaking in tongues, or "glossolalia," is believed by Christians to be—if genuine—a gift of God. Advocates of the reincarnation theory tend to regard it as a sign of some previous existence.

7

The Evidence for Reincarnation

In 1962 Professor Ian Stevenson met a young Lebanese who told him that in his home village of Kornayel there were several children who remembered previous incarnations. He gave Stevenson a letter of introduction to his brother. Two years later Stevenson had an opportunity to visit Lebanon and follow up his interest in reincarnation. He was able to investigate personally the curious case of Imad Elawar, and he tells the fascinating story in an article entitled "Twenty Cases Suggestive of Reincarnation," published in 1966. Imad was born in Kornayel in 1958. As soon as he began to talk, he repeatedly mentioned the

Right: in this 19th-century French painting, ghosts of warriors who died for their countries are depicted entering Heaven, where they are welcomed not by St. Peter but by the legendary Gaelic warrior Ossian. Many cases of apparent reincarnation involve people who died violently, often in battle. Assuming reincarnation to be possible, perhaps the shock of sudden death leaves a vivid memory that is likely to remain with the reincarnated spirit, and so make recall of a previous existence relatively probable.

"Suddenly he rushed up to a stranger in the street and hugged him"

names "Jamile" and "Mahmoud," although no members of his family had such names. He also talked about Khriby, a village some 30 kilometers from Kornayel across the mountains. One day when he was two years old, he was out for a walk with his grandmother. Suddenly he rushed up to a stranger in the street and hugged him. The bewildered man asked, "Do you know me?" and little Imad answered, "Yes, you were my neighbor." It turned out that the stranger was from Khriby.

Though the Elawar family belonged to an Islamic sect that believes in reincarnation, Imad's father did not like the suggestion that his son was a reincarnate. He became angry when Imad talked about his previous life in Khriby and said he belonged to the Bouhamzy family. So the boy suppressed such talk in his father's presence, but continued to tell his mother and grandparents about his memories. He talked a great deal about the beauty of Jamile. He mentioned an accident in which a man had had both his legs crushed beneath the wheels of a truck, and had died soon afterward. He remembered the accident very vividly, he said, but he had not been the man who was killed. This statement was puzzling, because as Imad grew older he repeatedly expressed delight in the fact that he was able to walk. He also repeatedly begged his parents to take him to Khriby, but his father refused.

When Professor Stevenson arrived in Kornayel, Imad was just over five years old, and had been describing memories of his former life for the past three years. He had never left the village. Stevenson collected all the facts he could. He talked to members of Imad's family and to Imad himself. Among other information, the boy gave him a detailed description of the house he had lived in in Khriby. Stevenson then traveled the rough mountain road to Khriby to check the information he had received.

He soon learned that Bouhamzy was the name of a local family, and that in 1943 Said Bouhamzy had been run over by a truck, had both his legs crushed, and had died after an unsuccessful operation. He was shown the house where Said had lived, but it did not correspond with Imad's description of his former home, nor did the facts he managed to learn about Said's life match Imad's memories of his previous existence.

Stevenson continued his investigations, however, and discovered that Said had had a cousin and close friend named Ibrahim Bouhamzy. Ibrahim had scandalized the village by openly living with his mistress, the beautiful young Jamile. His happiness had been short, though. In 1949 at the age of 25, he had died of tuberculosis. He had spent the last six months of his life bedridden and unable to walk, which had distressed him greatly. Like his cousin Said, Ibrahim had been a truck driver. He had himself been involved in a couple of accidents, and he had never gotten over Said's death. Mahmoud was the name of an uncle of Ibrahim.

On his first visit to Khriby, Stevenson was also able to confirm that the house Ibrahim had lived in matched Imad's description, and that the man who lived in the neighboring house was the person Imad had embraced on the street in Kornayel three years before. In all, Stevenson on this visit confirmed that out of 47 facts Imad had given him about his previous life, a total of 44 matched exactly with facts about the life of Ibrahim Bouhamzy.

Left: Professor Ian Stevenson, an American physician and professor of psychiatry who has contributed to several branches of parapsychology and written a book entitled *Twenty Cases Suggestive of Reincarnation*, based on his own research into the subject.

Below: this ancient Indian board game, similar to Snakes and Ladders, is called The Game of Heaven and Hell and is based on the Hindu concept of reincarnation.

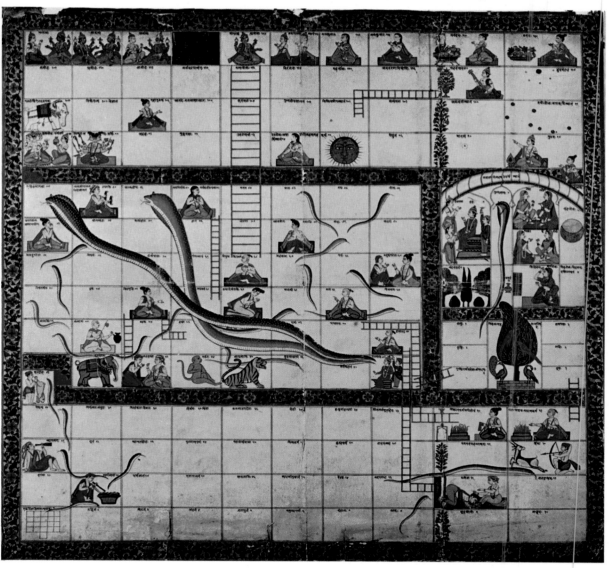

The Golden One

In 1865, in India, Jayaram Banerji and his wife Sundari had a son whom they named Haranath. His birth had been preceded by a strange clair-voyant dream of his father's, involving a *sadhu*, or holy man; and early in his life the young Haranath showed signs of pos-sessing strange powers. He fre-quently went into trances. Later, he experienced astral travel and claimed to com-municate with divine beings. He was widely venerated for his healing and for his ob-viously sincere love of God.

One day in 1896 Haranath was about to begin a journey when he suddenly lost con-sciousness. Ten hours later he still lay inert; his heart had stopped beating and all other signs of life had disappeared. His traveling companions made plans for his cremation.

Then he suddenly returned to consciousness. During his coma he had in fact been experiencing intense mental activity. He had been in communion with a "Great Being," whom he had seen once before as a child. This being was a 16th-century saint called Gouranga. While Haranath lay unconscious, the spirit of the saint was absorbed into his body.

After this experience, Haran-ath's complexion took on a golden hue (Gouranga means "the golden one").

He returned to Kornayel and persuaded Imad's father to let him take the boy to Khriby. The three of them went, and during the drive Imad produced seven correct statements about the route, which he had never traveled before. In Khriby, Imad pro-duced a further 16 facts about Ibrahim's life and his home, and Stevenson was able to confirm 14 of these as completely correct. Ibrahim's house had been locked up for several years and was opened especially for their visit, so Stevenson was able to check immediately statements that Imad made about its furnishings. In his former life as Ibrahim, the boy said, he had owned two rifles, one of them double-barreled. This proved to be correct, and when they entered the house he was able to go directly to a place where Ibrahim had hidden one of the rifles.

Stevenson has collected reports of over 1000 cases that are, as he cautiously puts it, "suggestive of reincarnation." The Imad Elawar case is one of the strongest, not just because of the quantity of corroborative evidence, but also because of the circumstances in which the evidence was obtained. Stevenson stumbled upon the case by a lucky chance. He arrived in Kornayel unannounced and began his investigation immediately, so there could be no question of fraud or deception because such an elaborate hoax would have taken some time to set up. Nor could there be any question of misconstruing and subsequently distorting the child's information to match the verification, consciously or uncon-sciously. In this case Stevenson collected the facts at first hand and not by hearsay, and wrote them down before attempting veri-fication.

There seems to be no doubt that, for whatever reason, the mind of the child Imad Elawar contained memories and impres-sions that corresponded with experiences in the life of the dead Ibrahim Bouhamzy. Whether this suggests that Imad was a re-incarnation of Bouhamzy is, of course, another question.

Left: the Hindu god Vishnu, shown in his third incarnation as the Boar Varaha. In this incarn-ation he killed a demon called Hiranyakashipu and rescued the earth goddess from the ocean into which the demon had thrown her.

Right: this 18th-century Tibetan painting is based on a text called the *Ch'os-nyid Bar-do*, which de-scribes the third of several trans-itional stages undergone by the soul after death and before re-birth. The painting shows the advent of the peaceful deities that appear at this stage, which is called "Experiencing Reality."

129

Belief in reincarnation is fundamental in the Hindu and Buddhist religions, so it is not surprising that some of the classic cases on record come from India. In 1961 and again in 1964 Stevenson visited the village of Rasulpur in Uttar Pradesh, India, to interview people and collect facts that might corroborate an apparent reincarnation case that had been brought to his attention. In 1954 a child of the village, Jasbir Jat, had fallen ill with smallpox at the age of three and a half, and had apparently died. Preparations for burial were made, but the child began to show faint signs of life. Some weeks passed before he was fully recovered, and when he was able to express himself clearly again, Jasbir spoke and behaved in a manner that distressed his family. He insisted that his name was Sobha Ram and that he was the son of a Brahmin,

Left: a wooden figure of the chief lama of Bhutan. According to some sects of Buddhism, the chief lamas of the monasteries are Bodhisattvas, or seekers of enlightenment on their way to becoming Buddhas, and are reincarnated in the same status—that is, as potential chief lamas—that they occupied in the former life. Below: a Buddhist New Year dance in Sikkim celebrating rebirth.

Shankar Lil Tyagi, of the village of Vehedi, which is about 20 miles from Rasulpur. He introduced into his speech sophisticated words characteristic of the Brahmin caste, and he refused to eat his family's food. Fortunately, a Brahmin woman heard about him and volunteered to cook Brahmin food for him.

This situation continued for several years. Communication between the villages of Rasulpur and Vehedi were virtually non-existent. In 1957, however, a Vehedi woman who had been born in Rasulpur paid a visit to her home village. She had not been back since 1952, when Jasbir was only 18 months old, but he recognized her. From others she learned the story of his strange claim and behavior, which she repeated to her own family when she returned to Vehedi. When the family of the late Sobha Ram Tyagi heard about it, they paid a visit to Rasulpur to meet Jasbir. The child greeted them all by name, showing that he knew the relationship of each to Sobha Ram and many facts about their life in Vehedi. He also gave an exact account of how Sobha Ram had died, which was as a result of a fall from a carriage during a marriage procession. After the visit, Jasbir was allowed to go to Vehedi several times and stay with the Tyagi family. He was much happier than in Rasulpur, and showed intimate familiarity with the family life and past history.

When Stevenson investigated this case he did not have the good fortune he had had in the Imad Elawar case of being present when the verifications took place. But by visiting the two villages and talking to the people involved he compiled a list of 39 facts about Sobha Ram's life that Jasbir had mentioned before he paid his first visit to Vehedi. Of these, 38 could be corroborated. The one that could not be verified was the most intriguing of all. Jasbir stated that Sobha Ram's fatal fall had been caused because he had been poisoned, and he even named the murderer. There was no way of proving this, but Stevenson discovered that the Tyagi family had suspected that Sobha Ram had been murdered. Furthermore, he found that the time of Sobha Ram's death had coincided with the time of Jasbir's smallpox illness, during which he too had almost died.

In a significant number of apparent reincarnation cases the previous life ended violently or prematurely. Believers maintain that this does not mean that only those that meet violent deaths are reincarnated, but simply that those who die a natural death, particularly in old age, do not carry over distinct memories from one life to another. Violent death, it seems, can leave strong impressions not only on the soul, but also in some cases on the physical body. Several researchers have noted birthmarks in alleged reincarnates situated where fatal wounds were apparently sustained in the previous life.

Guy Playfair quotes such a case in his book *The Flying Cow*. It is from the records of the Brazilian Institute for Psycho-Biophysical Research and concerns a woman named Tina. She was born in the town of Araraquara, 175 miles from São Paulo, and still works there as a lawyer with a public utility company. Tina is an unusual reincarnate in that as an adult today she clearly remembers incidents from her previous life. Normally such memories fade in childhood.

Tina remembers that she lived in France and that her name

The Bullet Marks

Tina was born in 1940 in Brazil, but she has clear memories of a previous existence as a child in France and of her own murder by a German soldier early in World War II. She gave an account of her death to the Brazilian Institute for Psychical Research.

"I don't think there was anyone at home that day," she wrote, "because it was I who answered the door. It must have been about 10 in the morning and the weather was cloudy." A soldier entered, wearing a round helmet and olive-green uniform. He carried what looked like a rifle and fired it at her heart.

"I remember," she continued, "asking for water before I died, but I don't remember if they gave me any. I can see myself lying on the floor on my back, wearing a light dress. I don't remember seeing any blood."

Tina has had from birth two distinct marks, on the front and back of her left side, precisely where a bullet aimed at the heart would have gone in and out. She has other memories too. In the interval between her death in France and her rebirth in Brazil she was present in the house of her parents-to-be. As soon as she could talk she correctly described all the furnishings in the house before her birth.

131

Above: the Greek philosopher and mathematician Pythagoras lived from 580 to 500 B.C. He claimed, however, that he had lived other lives: once as a Trojan warrior named Euphorbus who was slain during the Trojan War, once as a prophet named Hermotimus who was burned to death by his rivals, once as a Thracian peasant, once as the wife of a shopkeeper in Lydia, and once as a Phoenician prostitute. His doctrine of the transmigration of souls was only one of his mystical teachings.

was Alex Amadado Barralouf. Her father's name was Jean Paris and her mother's Angala. She believes that she came from the town of Vichy, and remembers shopping with her mother, a tall, blonde, well-dressed woman. When she was two and a half years old she recalls being taken to Le Havre and seeing the ships tied up on the quay. She learned French easily and has a strong sense of identification with France. She detests everything German because she believes she had been shot and killed by a German soldier during World War II. On the front and back of her left side are two marks that she has had from birth. They correspond with the positions that would have been marked if a bullet aimed at her heart had gone in and out.

Family anecdotes such as this one cannot be regarded as providing the same kind of evidence as Professor Stevenson's scrupulously objective investigations. But they are common in parts of the world where reincarnation is widely believed in, and they give an interesting insight into the belief.

Although belief in reincarnation is far less frequently found in the contemporary Western world, most people at some time have had a strange type of experience that is sometimes explained by the idea of reincarnation. This experience is generally known by the French term *déjà vu* which means "already seen." It refers to those instances in which a person has a strong feeling of having been in a place or a situation before. Various psychological explanations have been put forward to account for this. It has been suggested that the experience is a hallucination, or that it is an evocation of a memory that seemed to have been completely forgotten. Physiological explanations have also been advocated. One is that the brain receives two visual signals from the retina within a split second of each other, and that the so-called memory is implanted by the first of these two signals.

Although such explanations may be relevant to many ephemeral and rather vague sensations of *déjà vu*, they do not explain cases in which detailed knowledge, which could not have been acquired by normal means, is possessed. An example is if a person visiting a place for the first time can correctly describe present or former features of the town or landscape before actually seeing them.

Nils Jacobson, a Swedish psychiatrist, cites the following case in his book *Life Without Death?*, published in English in 1974. A patient had from time to time experienced throughout his adult life a kind of trance vision in which he was a World War I soldier who met his death in Flanders. The experience was always preceded by a sensation of profound depression and dullness, and began with an OOBE. He felt himself leave his body and glide out "into a milky-white, dense mist where everything was deathly silent." Then he was on a crowded railroad

Right: *The Morning of Sedgemoor* recalls the last battle fought on English soil, in the Duke of Monmouth's attempt to gain the throne. Left: Edward Ryall, who remembers being slain in this battle after a previous life as Somerset farmer John Fletcher. His book *Second Time Round* depicts 17th-century life in minute detail and contains obscure facts about people and places that have been verified—such as his recollection of brilliant northern lights before the battle.

Left: Christian Henry Heinecken, the "Infant of Lubeck," who shortly after his birth in 1721 began to speak fluently. By the age of one year he knew all of the Bible; by the age of four he had learned Latin and French. He died before reaching the age of five. Proponents of the reincarnation theory cite cases of child prodigies in support of the theory, suggesting that the astonishing faculties are an inheritance from a former life. Below: Mozart as a child performing with his father and his sister Nannerl. The greatest musical prodigy in history, Mozart was already composing music at the age of five.

station with a lot of soldiers amid great scenes of emotion and distress as relatives said goodby to the men embarking for the front. When he was aboard the train he hung out of the window, clasping the hands of a pretty young woman who gazed desperately into his eyes and whispered repeatedly, "Marcel, o mon Marcel," to which he replied, "Catherine, ma Cathy. . . ." Then the train pulled away and he experienced a long clattering journey through the dark. Finally the train arrived at a destination that he learned was near Arras. With hordes of other soldiers he disembarked and trudged through rain and mud to an encampment near the front line.

Time passed—he couldn't tell how long—and a day came when it was the turn of his company to attempt to take a village by storm on a height in front of them. He wormed his way with other soldiers along the trough of a deep ravine at the bottom of which a stream flowed. This afforded the only protected approach to the village. They finally arrived at the point from which the attack was to be launched, and at a given signal he went over the top and ran toward the village, which he saw clearly in front of him. He was suddenly stopped by a powerful blow and burning pain in his chest, and everything went blank.

Jacobson's patient had experienced this harrowing vision several times before 1966 when, during a journey, he found himself near Arras. He decided to take the opportunity to discover whether the vision had any foundation in reality. He drove into and around the town, but everything was unfamiliar. Then he came to a crossroads and saw a signpost with the name "Bapaume," and his heart rose in his throat. About three miles down that road he began to recognize features, and when they arrived at the village his recall became crystal clear. He was able to take his family through the maze of narrow streets to a field. There he pointed out the winding ravine from which rose steep slopes toward another village beyond, the place where in his vision he had died. When they went to this village he was disappointed to find it unfamiliar. Neither the church nor the buildings were as in his vision. But his son, by chatting to an elderly inhabitant, learned that the village had been completely destroyed during violent fighting between French and German forces in November 1914, and that the church and the buildings around it had been rebuilt in the 1930s.

This case is interesting not only because the subject had told others about his vision before some of its details were confirmed, but also because others were present at the time of verification. *Déjà vu* is not normally preceded by a visionary experience that the person consciously remembers, and cases in which paranormally obtained knowledge is communicated to another before the event are rare. This may partly be, however, because people are reluctant to communicate such apparently baseless information for fear of being proved wrong and thought foolish.

A 26-year-old German woman recorded a strange *déjà vu* experience in 1967. Her husband became impatient with her when, during a journey by car through a part of Germany which neither had previously visited, she suddenly exclaimed that she knew the area because she had lived there before. Although he knew that it was the first time she had been in that part of the

Above: the French mathematician, scientist, and philosopher Blaise Pascal (1623-62). His brilliant mind was evident in childhood, but his early education consisted almost entirely of literature. The boy taught himself geometry, and at the age of 11 discovered a new geometrical system. The following year he wrote a treatise on the subject of acoustics.

Left: the English novelist Joan Grant, who has recalled memories of several previous lives and has put them into her books. Although classified as novels, they are regarded by her as autobiographies.

Right: an ancient Egyptian wall-painting showing a group of maidens. When she visited Egypt, Joan Grant was overcome by a flood of memories, which she used as a basis for her book *Winged Pharaoh*. In the book she describes her life as Sekeeta, an Egyptian princess.

Below right: a wall-painting in a house in Pompeii showing part of an initiation ceremony of the cult of Dionysus. It was in Pompeii a few years ago, that a Brazilian woman discovered the familiar features of a previous life that had haunted her for years. Born into an upper-class family, Celia (whose story is told in Guy Playfair's book *The Indefinite Boundary*) showed signs of sexual precociousness even in childhood, and throughout her life suffered from vividly violent, recurring dreams. In middle age she visited Pompeii, and recognized it at once. She led her companions to "her" house, which turned out to have been the house with the wall-painting shown in the photograph— and formerly the city's brothel.

country, she insisted that it was familiar to her. She pointed out a house where, she said, she had lived with her parents and two brothers in a previous life when her name had been Maria D. They stopped at a village tavern and she immediately recognized the proprietor as someone who, when much younger, had served her family. This finally made her husband wonder whether her talk had been more than mere fantasy, and he casually inquired of the old man about the "D. family." The parents, the older son, and the daughter were all dead, he told them sadly, and the death of "poor little Maria" had been most tragic. She had been savagely kicked to death by a horse in a stable. This information awakened what seemed like vivid and terrifying memories in the wife, who broke down and cried as she recalled the details of her previous death.

All the cases we have looked at are, in Stevenson's phrase, "suggestive of reincarnation." But there may be other explanations. The first that springs to mind is that they are all due to fraud or some sort of delusion. However, there are too many anecdotes and too many carefully investigated cases on record for this easy solution to be acceptable. The only other explana-

tion that seems at all tenable is that the alleged memories of former lives are acquired by extrasensory perception.

Modern parapsychological research has established fairly conclusively that telepathy, clairvoyance, and precognition do take place, particularly in heightened states of consciousness. It is theoretically possible that information in the mind of any living person may be paranormally acquired by another, or that past, present, or future events or scenes can be clairvoyantly experienced. But the conditions that normally facilitate ESP, such as the existence of a bond between sender and receiver, or circumstances of crisis, or the development of a general psychic faculty, are not to be found in the experiences described in this chapter. None of the subjects had any connection with or prior knowledge of the deceased, and none of them showed any ability to acquire information paranormally about any other facts except those about their former life experience. Imad and Jasbir had no knowledge of events in Khriby and Vehedi after the deaths of Ibrahim and Sobha Ram, and the knowledge that they possessed had a continuity and coherence that suggests the functioning of memory rather than ESP. ESP tends to supply fragmentary and discontinuous information, and to mix information received from the external source with contents of the consciousness of the receiver. The ESP hypothesis is also inadequate to explain the existence of, for example, birthmarks on the skin of an alleged reincarnate that correspond exactly with wounds received in an alleged previous life. Nor can it account for sustained creative work such as, for example, the extraordinary novels of Joan Grant.

Joan Grant was born in England in 1907, and as a child became aware that she possessed memories of previous lives in other centuries and other lands. Her claims were an embarrassment to her family, and she did not fully develop her psychic gifts until adulthood, when a visit to Egypt brought a flood of intense and detailed memories of that land in ancient times. She wrote down the memories as they came to her, which made a great deal of fragmentary material. With the cooperation of her husband, a psychiatrist, she put the fragments into a novel that was published in 1937 under the title *Winged Pharaoh*. She had done no research before or while writing the book, which was presented as the story of the life of Sekeeta, the daughter of an Egyptian pharaoh who had lived 3000 years ago. When scholars, critics, and Egyptologists evaluated the novel, they unanimously praised the accuracy of its historical detail, though they were understandably dubious about Joan Grant's claim that her accuracy was due to the fact that she *was* Sekeeta. Other books followed, and in her autobiography, *Far Memory*, she wrote: "During the last 20 years, seven books of mine have been published as historical novels which to me are biographies of previous lives I have known." It is a seemingly outlandish claim, but to attempt to apply the ESP hypothesis to the Joan Grant case only produces the scarcely less fantastic explanation that she acquired her information by telepathically picking the minds of Egyptian scholars unknown to her, and focusing and sustaining her telepathic powers in a manner without precedent in ESP research.

When all the evidence has been examined, it seems that the ancient and widespread belief in reincarnation offers an explanation for many otherwise incomprehensible occurrences. Hindus and Buddhists, among others, believe that a single human lifetime is only one stage in the development of a soul, which has to return to Earth many times in many different bodies before it can attain perfection. They believe that a person's actions generate a force known as *karma*, which determines his destiny in the next existence. If the soul brings with it into life an accumulation of bad karma acquired through wrong action in a previous life, it will have to spend a lifetime expiating it in order to advance its process of growth. Such a belief accounts for the apparent injustices and inequalities of earthly life. It explains differences of personality and endowment, precocity in some children and special gifts in people of genius. And it serves, as no other philosophical or religious concept does, to reconcile man to his fate while at the same time encouraging him to change himself. It also may account for many of the strange memories described in this chapter. It is a belief that is surely worthy of more serious consideration than it has been given.

Above: Dr. Nils Jacobson, a Swedish psychiatrist who has made an extensive study of cases of apparent reincarnation. One of his patients recalled in great detail harrowing events from a previous life when he fought as a soldier in World War I. In Jacobson's opinion, testimonies of reincarnation to date point strongly to the hypothesis of survival and life beyond death.

Right: a Tibetan painting showing the Wheel of Life, which represents in pictorial form the basic principles of Tibetan Buddhism. The sages of the East have long believed in the idea of survival after death, and western scientists are at last beginning to investigate the concept seriously.

Are There Other Worlds?

When Robert Bruce saw a stranger writing on a slate in the captain's cabin, far out at sea, he may have been tempted to think that he was having a hallucination. But the writing on the slate remained to convince him of the reality of what he had seen, and his conviction persuaded the captain to obey the slate message and change course. By these means a ship in distress was rescued. Bruce, to his amazement, was able to identify one of the passengers as the stranger in the cabin. On examining the stranger's handwriting, it was found to be identical with that on the slate. But perhaps what was most puzzling of all, the passenger had no recollection of his astral journey. He had merely dreamed that he was on board a ship that was coming to rescue them. How many other psychic journeys might have taken place, and remained unknown to the person experiencing them because no evidence such as this was presented?

Ancient accounts of astral exploits include that of Hermotimus, the Greek mystic of the 6th century B.C., who frequently left his body. Another concerns the prophet Elisha, whose psychic powers ensured the safety of his people according to the Bible. It is difficult to judge the quality of the evidence in these ancient cases. We can only surmise that certain strange things must have taken place in order to create such strong legends. But the more we delve into stories such as these, the less totally fantastic they seem. Equally puzzling powers have been claimed by modern astral projectors. In addition, many ancient beliefs—such as the existence of the aura and the system of the subtle body used in acupuncture and Hindu mysticism—have received confirmation in modern scientific studies. Belief in the existence of a double extends from ancient to modern times. It has been vouched for by so many spectators, and in the case of the Canadian politician Charles Good, even by photography, that it is impossible for it to be dismissed merely as the product of a nervous or unstable temperament. Either the projection of the double is a feasible occurrence, or else people in totally different places and with no knowledge of each other take part in some kind of collective hallucination. Either solution must make us question our normal everyday grasp of reality.

The strange experiences of skilled astral projectors such as Sylvan Muldoon, Oliver Fox, or Robert Monroe may, at first, seem too incredible, but scientific experiments by psychic researchers have suggested that these accounts should be taken seriously. Whether or not it is astral projection, it is evident that some sort of psychic experience takes place. Out-of-the-body experiences, if that is what they are, seem to have different functions. Some appear to be purely exploratory, acquainting the astral projector with new and different states of consciousness that exist outside the physical body. Others seem to have a definite healing or rescuing purpose, such as that of the child Max Hoffman, who came to his mother for help when he had been buried while in a coma. Still others seem to act as a release from intolerable situations, such as the case of Ed Morrell, who was being brutally tortured by prison guards. The most striking experiences have often occurred to those hovering on the brink of death. George Ritchie, during the nine minutes in which onlookers believed him to have died, underwent an extraordinary religious illumination accompanied by a vision of other worlds. Lord Geddes describes the sense of freedom attained as the physical consciousness deteriorates and the ego is released into new multidimensional Universes that blend into each other.

The phenomena of possession and reincarnation also hint that there may be elements in our world which for the most part we are unaware of. How could the totally untutored Chico Xavier produce so many learned books on subjects that he knew nothing about? How could Lurancy Vennums have acquired enough personal knowledge of Mary Roff to convince Mary's parents that Mary's spirit inhabited her body? Where did Rosemary receive her communications in ancient Egyptian from? How did a child such as Imad Alawar get such detailed information of events and people outside his environment, most of which could be checked and corroborated?

Reincarnation, astral projection, possession, the subtle body—are these all manifestations of other realities beyond our normal comprehension? Are there other worlds coexisting with our own, but on a different time scale? Or is our own life a fragment of some far greater scheme whose existence is only hinted at by strange memories and psychic experiences?

For centuries all over the world people have believed that the physical body is only one kind of reality. From primitive cultures to sophisticated religions the idea has persisted that the human spirit is in some way independent of the body, that it will survive after death, and in certain cases during life—in sleep or trance—that it may detach itself from the physical shell. Western science has tended to deride such notions, but has produced no proof against them. Many people have experienced other states of consciousness and other levels of reality, and even the skeptic must take account of those instances in which information has been produced that could not have been acquired by normal means.

We all have a tendency either to ignore what we cannot explain, or search for a solution that will provide all the answers. There may not be enough evidence to prove conclusively that other realities exist. There is certainly enough for the belief to be examined seriously. Perhaps we possess only the merest clues to other dimensions, but if such clues provoke our questioning, that is at least a start.

Picture Credits